D1594155

Cosmographical Glasses

Cosmographical Glasses

Geographic Discourse, Gender,
and Elizabethan Fiction

CONSTANCE C. RELIHAN

The Kent State University Press
KENT AND LONDON

© 2004 by The Kent State University Press, Kent, Ohio 44242
ALL RIGHTS RESERVED
Library of Congress Catalog Card Number 2004010054
ISBN 0-87338-811-9
Manufactured in the United States of America

08 07 06 05 04   5 4 3 2 1

A version of a portion of chapter 2, "The Gendered and Geographic 'Glasses' of the English Novella," appeared as "Disordinate Desire and the Construction of Geographic Otherness in the Early Modern Novella" in *Prose Fiction and Early Modern Sexualities in England, 1570–1640*, ed. Constance C. Relihan and Goran V. Stanivukovic (New York: Palgrave Macmillan, 2003), 43–59.

LIBRARY OF CONGRESS CATALOGING-IN-PUBLICATION DATA
Relihan, Constance Caroline.
    Cosmographical glasses : geographic discourse, gender, and Elizabethan fiction / Constance C. Relihan.
        p.   cm.
    Includes bibliographical references and index.
    ISBN 0-87338-811-9 (hardcover : alk. paper)
    1. English fiction—Early modern, 1500–1700—History and criticism. 2. Geographical discoveries in literature. 3. Women and literature—England—History—16th century. 4. Pastoral fiction, English—History and criticism. 5. America—In literature. 6. Geography in literature. 7. Ethnicity in literature. 8. Sex role in literature. I. Title.
    PR839.G46R45 2004
    823'.30932—dc22   2004010054

British Library Cataloging-in-Publication data are available.

For Tom, Maeve, and Meg

Contents

Acknowledgments

I owe debts of gratitude to many, many people. During the years in which I worked on this project, I benefited greatly from research support I have received from Auburn University and Auburn's Department of English. My colleagues' support has been equally valuable and stimulating: I have been fortunate to have individuals who have been willing to listen to me talk, often at too great length, about sixteenth-century fiction and the implications of its geography. I have also been lucky enough to have students whose interest in my work has propelled me forward; in particular, I would like to thank Beth Calhoun and Patsy Fowler for taking time out from their writing to ask about mine.

I have also benefited from the support and knowledge of the growing group of scholars working on early modern prose fiction. In particular, I would like to thank Goran Stanivukovic, Lori Humphrey Newcomb, Derek Alwes, and Terry Prendergast for reading early portions of this manuscript and providing extremely important e-mail support. I am also grateful to those individuals who provided me with feedback at the various conferences at which I discussed the importance of geography to sixteenth-century fiction: their generosity and good humor have encouraged me immeasurably. I continue to be thankful as well for the support of Arthur Kinney and Shirley Nelson Garner.

As we all know, there is a very fine line between our professional personae and our personal lives. I owe significant debts to those friends here in Auburn who form my community: their help in difficult times and their exuberant support in times of celebration have been a boon that I could not have imagined. In particular, I would like to thank the group of academic parents on whom my husband and I lean.

This study is about the link between place and gender. My thinking about it has been profoundly influenced by two women who passed away before my work on it could be completed. My mother, Mary Ann Oberhauser Relihan, and my mother-in-law, Alice McGreal O'Shea, both provided me with love, support, and an awareness of how strong women could be and how integrally linked women and location are. Their deaths have forever changed the places I call "home."

Finally, I owe immeasurable personal and professional gratitude to my husband, Tom O'Shea, and to our daughters, Maeve and Margaret Ann. Their love and belief in me have given me the energy to pursue this study; their sacrifices have made it possible for me to complete it. They define for me the most important space I inhabit.

Introduction

If it form the one landscape that we, the inconstant ones,
    Are consistently homesick for, this is chiefly
Because it dissolves in water.
. . . .
What could be more like Mother or a fitter background
    For her son, the flirtatious male who lounges
Against a rock in the sunlight, never doubting
    That for all his faults he is loved; whose works are but
Extensions of his power to charm? From weathered outcrop
    To hill-top temple, from appearing waters to
Conspicuous fountains, from a wild to a formal vineyard,
    Are ingenious but short steps that a child's wish
To receive more attention than his brothers, whether
    By pleasing or teasing, can easily take.
        —W. H. Auden, "In Praise of Limestone," ll. 1–3, 11–20

Auden's "In Praise of Limestone" has long baffled me, yet thinking about
the subject of the following study gives me insight into its complexity. What
could be more like mother than limestone, simultaneously a clearly defined,
substantial, solid, lived-in space and a dissolvable entity marked by a "secret
system of caves and conduits" (l. 5). Auden's limestone figures forth both
the physical, geographic certainty—the "homeland" we desire—and the
impossibility of clinging to a solid, unchanging substance. Like the locations of early modern prose fiction, the rock of Auden's poem represents
the maternal body—the lived-in de Certeauian "space" that Elizabethan

prose fiction writers tried to develop to authorize their tales within ethno-graphic discourse—and the threats posed to its identity by the overwhelm-ingly chameleonic quality of ethnographic discourse itself.

The discourse of place that the early modern geographers and ethnog-raphers inherited from the medieval world provided solid means by which writers of fictions—be they novellas or Arcadian, Heliodoran, or middle-class romances—could assert a useful nationalistic and religious purpose for their texts. As early modern travelers, explorers, and merchants brought back observation-based reports that could amplify and qualify earlier ac-counts, fiction writers found new uses for their texts; they too could be part of the new movement to describe, explain, and colonize. These fictional texts, however, like Auden's poem, cannot help but gender that experience of space. The definition of space is inevitably and implicitly for writers of early modern prose a definition of gender relations. Struggles to define cultures and spaces become struggles to control female sexuality and re-production; they become struggles about mothers, be they motherlands, mother tongues, or the mother church; virgins who could become moth-ers, like the *Ciceronis Amor*'s Terentia; or women who are already mothers, like *Pandosto*'s Bellaria. The writers of the texts we will consider all attempt to define the spaces of their texts in order to control and categorize their, and their culture's, relationship with non-English places in an effort to iden-tify for themselves what it means to be male and English and Elizabethan. Such an attempt, patriarchal in the strictest sense of the word, necessarily means engaging in discourse that controls and categorizes the objects against which it projects itself—foreign cultures and women.

I did not set out to write a study on gender. I began—a ridiculously long time ago, it seems—with a fairly narrow interest in how Turks were repre-sented in early prose fiction. However, at every juncture I found myself faced with the awareness that, for the texts I study, gender difference and geo-graphical difference are inseparable. Places and cultures are defined in op-position to each other in early modern romances by how the women in these texts are victimized or empowered or, more typically, victimized while seeming to be empowered. The study grew then from a simple inquiry into the fictional representation of cultural difference to a more complex analy-sis of the creation of oppositional categories, of the roots of colonial op-pression and the ways in which the discourse of colonization and the dis-course of patriarchy have been intertwined in early modern discourse. It is only through understanding the complexities of this interweaving that we can hope to detangle them for those who come after us.

The intermingling of Elizabethan fiction and geographic and ethnographic discourse is the subject of this study, for these prose narratives are uniquely positioned generically and historically to make the greatest use of the burgeoning market for travel narratives as a means to catch the reader's attention and influence the reading experience. The opening moments of Henry Robarts's *Honours Conquest* (1598) and *Pheander the Mayden Knight* (1595) provide an example of the ways in which fiction and geographical thinking are uniquely conjoined in early modern prose fiction.[1] *Honours Conquest* is a romance about the crusades of Edward of Lancaster. In defending his choice of subject to his readers, Robarts writes:

> And if any will alleage, that in this Poeticall praising of him, there be many fictions (as, *Poetis et pictoribus per magna conceditur licentia*) let such learne to reade those manner of bookes, as Socrates wished women to vse their looking glasses; namely, faire women, to looke on their glasses, to beware that their good maners may shine as well as their beautie; and ill-fauoured women, to indeuour that their inward vertues might make gratious theyr outward deformities. So let Gentlemen by reading these bookes obserue therein onelye those things, the practise whereof may innoble them more and more, and the baser and cowardly sort, here learne only what may promote them. (3–4)

Although this is an utterly conventional opening, it links some of the major issues that will concern us. The historical figure—an eleventh-century crusader—is to become a romance hero whose adventures throughout a range of foreign countries will assume a didactic value in creating the moral character of both the women and men who will encounter his text. His travels will become a "glasse" for women, helping them to improve their behavior so "their good maners may shine as well as their beautie," while simultaneously ennobling men and linking both genders of readers to the humanist tradition that Robarts's use of the untranslated Latin tag implies.

Robarts makes even more explicit the connections between fiction and geography in the dedicatory letters that precede *Pheander*. The first, to "the

Worshipfull Rawleigh Gilbert, Esq.," presents his dedicatee with "this Historie, written in my trauels at Sea, being sundry times employed by Gentlemen of honorable account, and famous for their seruices done" (3). Robarts,
in other words, explains his text as being in a sense the product of his geographical wanderings in service to experienced and esteemed mariners and
merchants. Although not explicitly stating that the romance he is about to
present is informed by the cultures he encountered on his travels, Robarts
lets his tale bask in the reflected glow of the geographical knowledge that
he has presumably obtained at sea.

A second letter, "to my beloued Country-men, the curteous Readers"
(4), transfers the geographical connections into the text itself:

> Gentlemen, after many bloudy bickerings and dangerous hazards in
> great perils on the seas, I haue recouered the hauen of my desire, and
> haue brought for your delight, this stranger Knight, a Prince borne. . . .
> Albeit my skill is not such as is required, yet haue I taken vpon me a
> Pilots charge, and in safety haue set him ashore, where his desire led
> him, vnto whom Gentiles, my hope is, your accustomed fauour to all
> strangers shall not be denied . . . after his long trauell with carefull
> trouble to delight you, receiue but the least shew of good liking, it is
> all hee expecteth: your courtesie is more then the cost, from which as
> your Englishmen and Gentiles allianate, so shall hee endeuour to
> deserue better, and shall in his trauell hereafter report of you as you
> are, & bind me his carefull Pilot, your Countryman, through whose
> procurement he is come hither, to your humble seruice. (4)

The author gains here a measure of exemplarity for his text in two ways:
first he emphasizes his identity as someone who knows firsthand the difficulties of travel and who might then, presumably, be able to present a narrative
of wandering with some accuracy; second, he presents himself to his readers (here exclusively male) as a "Pilot." His readers become, then, part of one
of the cultures that the wandering Pheander visits, and as the text progresses
and we are taken more and more into the narrator's confidence, we enjoy
some vicarious identification with the narrator. We become both a country
that the romance's hero visits and the narrator's confidant-coconspirator, helping to bring him there: the manipulation of geographic difference creates
both cultural difference and cultural assimilation. And as the dedicatory material from Robarts's texts suggests, the reading experience is affected both

by gender as well as geography.² Specific authorial or narratival asides to readers often construct the gender of the implied reader, altering our experience of early modern prose fiction and augmenting the tensions inherent in it. The struggle to differentiate oneself from the experience of fictional prose is dependent upon equally intense bonds of gender identification and alienation.

Another way of thinking about these tensions within early fiction is by reference to the distinction drawn by Michel de Certeau between "place" (*lieu*) and "space" (*espace*) in narrative discourse.³ "Place," in his argument, which has broad implications for sociology and cultural studies as well as literary studies, is an "instantaneous configuration of positions. It implies an indication of stability" (117). In other words, it is a geometrical, two-dimensional, formulaic, and synchronic identification of a location. "Space," as he puts it, "is a practiced place . . . composed of intersections of mobile evidence." It is "like the word when it is spoken, that is, when it is caught in the ambiguity of an actualization" (117). It is at least three-dimensional: it encompasses both the synchronic and diachronic axes of linguistic analysis as well as the heteroglossia of which Bakhtin speaks. This definition of space—of its simultaneous multiplicity of meaning—is, I think, essential for our developing a thorough understanding of the meanings of Elizabethan prose romance. Too often critical tendencies have dismissed these romances' locations as "places"—as static "configuration[s] of position[s]," as insignificant markers necessary within the texts only because all narratives must be set somewhere, or as simple markers differentiating the court and pastoral worlds. If, however, we are able to recover a sense of these locations as "spaces," we will recover a more thorough understanding of the complex ways in which these often geographically dismissed texts become "glasses" that reflect and refract the social and cultural realities of early modern England. We will be better equipped to understand the ways in which these texts reflect and critique the dominant ideological positions of their period. We will be better able to recognize the fantastic nature of the material presented to us and be better able to recognize the anomalies that the period's original readers would have recognized, which should alert us to the ways in which the often joyful conclusions of these romances are seriously undermined.

It is the presence of the ethnographic and geographic lens within the fiction that transforms the "places" of the texts' settings into "spaces." The complex resonances of the cultures within the minds of the original readers lift the simple allusion to place (e.g., the Bohemia and Sicilia of Robert Greene's *Pandosto*) off the page and change it into a multidimensional space through which we may glimpse a wide range of associations and connections. Through ethnographic understanding, settings become heteroglot. The heteroglossia is complicated by the competing claims of both the ethnographic texts and the fictions themselves. Because the ostensibly nonfictional texts are themselves an amalgam of received material, direct observation, and fantastic legend and because they purport both to describe fairly and to be monuments to the power and glory of a reformed Christian God, the voice with which they speak is complex, always at least double, and suggests a very sophisticated and involved reception on the part of its readers.

The tensions between spaces and places, for de Certeau, mark out tensions between what he calls "frontiers" and "bridges"; they "authorize the establishment, displacement, or transcendence of limits," and consequently "set in opposition within the closed field of discourse, two movements that intersect (setting and transgressing limits)" (123). These frontiers and bridges are explicitly seen in the ways in which the fiction engages questions of location and geographic difference. And because male and female experiences of travel during the early modern period differ—women are less likely to be the traveler than the reader of the travel report, and women are more likely to stand in for the exotic location the male traveler visits (becoming, to cite a famous example, John Donne's "new found land")—the geographical implications of these texts are significantly gendered as well.

The first chapter of this study examines the similarities between culturally and geographically didactic prose, which makes no overt claims to fictionality, and the analogous claims made by fictional prose texts, which make no claims to presenting factual narratives. It argues that both categories of text are engaged in the same cultural work: establishing foreign locations as de Certeauian "spaces" onto which cultural anxieties and the project of colonization may be projected under the guise of ethnographic and geographic didacticism.

The following chapters examine various kinds of ways in which fictional texts appropriate the spirit of ethnographic and geographic texts. The second chapter analyzes a number of novella collections and their appeals to historical and geographic factuality in order to examine the associations between the genre, the discourses of colonialism, and the construction of gender. It argues that within the novella anxieties about the dissolution of national cultures and identities are often linked to appeals to historical factuality, identifiable geographic "spaces," and violence against women. The following chapter focuses primarily on Robert Greene's *Pandosto: The Triumph of Time* (1588) and Laurence Twine's *The Patterne of Painefull Adventures* (1594?–1607), examining the ways in which historically identifiable geographical spaces, such as Bohemia and Sicily, and overtly fictional places, such as the "Trapalonia" of Greene's text or the "Machilenta" that appears in Twine's, are used to complicate the romances' representation of utopian fantasies, safely protecting patriarchal culture from female agency. A separate chapter treats the use of location within specifically Arcadian romance, examining how texts influenced by Sir Philip Sidney's romance—which claims that the adventures of its main characters would provide "full works to excellent geographers" (*Old Arcadia* 153)—demonstrate that even this most idyllic form of early fiction, which ostensibly resists identification of its settings with early modern historical realities, uses the discourses of geography and ethnography to promote the ends of European colonialism and English nationalism.

A final chapter examines the use of Latin with early modern prose romance as a kind of linguistic foreign country, especially for women readers deprived of the humanist education necessary for its interpretation. Centering primarily on Robert Greene's *Ciceronis Amor* (1589), which is presented by its prefatory material as a portion of Cicero's biography, which Plutarch and Cornelius Nepos excluded from their factual biographies, it studies the ways in which both appeals to biographical truth and to cultural difference use the non-native language to implicate early modern fiction in the use of cultural difference as a means of asserting and undermining claims about the nature of English society.

1

The Fiction of Ethnography /
The Ethnography of Fiction

To be brief, Gentlemen, I have seen the world and rounded it, though
not with travel yet with experience.
  —Robert Greene, preface to *A Notable Discovery of Cozenage* (1591)

They which go down to the sea in ships, and occupy the great waters,
they see the works of the Lord and his wonders in the deep.
  —Psalm 107:23–24, qtd. in Richard Hakluyt, *The Principal Navigations* (1589)

Thomas Blundeville, in the preface to his *Brief Description of Universal Maps
and Cards* (1589) observes that without geography "the necessarie reading of
Histories is halfe lame" (sig. A2ᵛ).¹ Yet, supplying that other leg—eliminat-
ing that limp—is considerably difficult. As the chapter epigraphs suggest,
recovering the texts that contain the material for which Blundeville calls
resists easy categorization. In fact, the attempt to identify the early modern
discourse of geographic place inevitably leads to what Homi Bhabha refers
to as the "slippage of categories" that is inherent in any attempt to create a
homogenized national narrative that disregards the complex nature of the
lived experience, the "locality" of a culture (140).² The discursive categories
that supply the geographic information Blundeville seeks—ethnography, car-
tography, chorography, history, traveler's tale—resist identification and separation in the early modern period even as they simultaneously provide a

means by which the prose of the period that transgresses the boundaries of these categories is made recognizable as fiction both to sixteenth-century and modern readers. Travel, as Greene and Hakluyt recognized, provides a basis for knowledge—both secular and divine—and for stories of marvels and of the everyday. Moreover, the tradition of such writings, dating back to Strabo and flourishing in the medieval period, combined the factual and the fictional even in ostensibly true narratives, creating texts that both assert and undercut their factual accuracy.

The early modern English ethnographic representation of foreign cultures is, above all, a fictional representation, and detangling the two narrative strands is challenging. "Every story is a travel story," writes Michel de Certeau; we might reverse that statement: every travel story is a story (115). Even when unacknowledged, the categories of fictional and historical report mesh. Medieval travel discourse had, as Margaret Hodgen reported in her very useful *Early Anthropology in the Sixteenth and Seventeenth Centuries,* combined "fragments of ancient learning and superstition, disfigured by careless repetition and invention" (34). Her assessment, however, suggests that the authors of early travel literature lacked concern for their texts, that it was carelessness rather than conscious design or a response to cultural imperatives that "disfigured" the texts and distanced them from a more useful ideal. She notes,

> Not only were the ancient names of ancient peoples confused but so also were their cultures. Several distinct groups were often lumped together as one. A description of a tribe in Asia was often applied, without explanation or apology, to one in Africa. Further, in the takeover of anthropological tradition from antiquity, the feeling for elapsed time was lost. Medieval scholarship seemed to have no realization that a people described by the ancients one thousand years before might no longer exist. (34)

Stephen Greenblatt is more blunt, acknowledging that for a range of reasons, both conscious and unconscious, early travel writers were "liars" (7), echoing the notion that every travel story is a story. Geographic accuracy and chronology, in other words, were often subordinate to drives toward narrative structure and the powerful use of details, and these drives emerged from the power of generic tradition. The tradition of what John Gillies refers to as "old" geography pushed geographic discourse toward the repetition of received anecdotes and fictional details even as an impulse toward a "new," observation-based geography emerged.[3] Diachronic and synchronic description collapse; observable data and received wisdom occupy the same space in the ethnographic texts of the period. This collapse, as this chapter will show, provides the groundwork for the construction of fictional texts imbued with a geographic sense, which build on geography to create fictional, colonized, gendered alterity.

Fictional Facts and Cosmographical Glasses: Reading Early Modern Geography

William Watreman's 1555 *The Fardle of Facions,* a translation of Johann Boemus's *Omnium gentium mores, leges, & ritus ex multis clarissimis rerum scriptoribus* (1520), presents one example of the complex ways in which fictional and ostensibly nonfictional representations merge within the period's ethnographic and geographic discourse.[4] In addition to being one of the earliest examples of what Gillies identifies both as "a common ethnographic text" and, elsewhere, as a "geographical classic" (93, 149), Boemus's text was popular, being revised in 1536 and subsequently appearing in twenty-three other editions in its original Latin as well as in French, Italian, English, and Spanish translations (Hodgen 132).[5]

Watreman's translation begins with Boemus's preface, which explains the nature of his work:

I haue sought out at times, as laisure hath serued me, Good reader, the maners and facio[n]s[,] the Lawes, Customes and Rites, of all suche peoples, as semed notable, and worthy to be put in remembra[n]ce, together with the situatio[n] [and] descriptio[n] of their habitatio[n]s: which the father of stories *Herodotus* the Greke, *Diodorus,* the Siciliane, *Berosus, Strabo, Solinus, Trogus Pompeius, Ptolomeus, Plinius, Cornelius* the still, *Dionysius* the Afri[c?]ane, *Po[m]ponius Mela, Caesar, Iosephus,* and certein of the later writers, as *Vincentius,* and *Aeneas Siluius* (whiche aftreward made Pope, had to name *Pius* the seconde) Anthonie *Sabellicus,* Ihon *Nauclerus,* Ambrose Calepine, Nicholas Perotte, in his *cornu copiae,* and many other famous writers eche one for their parte, as it ware skatered, [and] by piece meale, set further to posteritie. Those I saie haue I sought out, gathered together, and acordyng to the ordre of the storie and tyme, digested into this litle packe. (sig. A.i[r–v])

These two lengthy sentences reveal, it seems, the framework of the text: he has based his descriptions on the works, the "stories," of others, not on direct observation—on authorities rather than empirical evidence. He has participated in an established humanist tradition, having "shocked . . . vp together" (sig. A.iv) what he has culled from his sources; furthermore, he has organized his gleanings "accordyng to the ordre of the storie and tyme" as if compelled by motives that urge accuracy and narrative clarity. Nonetheless, the conclusion of the preface suggests a slightly different authorial plan. There he asserts that he has produced his text because

> there is in the knowledge of peoples, [and] of their maners and facions, so great pleasure and profite, and euery man cannot, yea, fewe men will, go traveile the countries themselues: me thinkes gentill reader, thou oughtest with muche thanke to receyue at my hande these bookes of the maners and facions of peoples most notable and famous, togyther with the places whiche thei enhabite: And with no lesse cherefulnes to embrase theim, then if beyng ledde on my hande from countrey to countrey, I should poynct the at eye, how euery people liueth, and where they haue dwelte, and at this daye doe. (sig. A.ix^v)

In other words, Boemus suggests, classical descriptions of cultures and geography are as accurate in the sixteenth century as they were when Strabo wrote his geography. Were we to visit the locations he describes, with Boemus as our guide, we would see what Strabo and his sources saw: the historical past of his sources and the contemporary experience of his readers merging under the influence of the "old" geography. If that is true, then why not just read Boemus's sources ourselves? Because, as he goes on to tell us, if we are criticized for reading his work because people think it is "a thyng hath bene written of, many yeares agone, and that by a thousand sondry menne, and yet he but borowyng their woordes, bryngeth it foorthe for a mayden booke, and named it his owne" (sig. A.ix^v), we should respond that Boemus has "not only brought thee other mennes old store, but opened thee also the treasury of myne owne witte and bokes, not euery where to be found, and like a liberall feaster haue set before thee much of myne owne, and many thynges newe" (sig. B.i^r). The work then is a combination of Boemus's reading and his wit—of material culled from his predecessors and from his own mind and thinking, of received knowledge and "realistic shadings."[6] Direct observation, even in this revised statement of his intentions, remains an untapped source of information.

My point here is not only to show that Watreman's translation of Boemus is partially fictionalized because it relies on traditional sources rather than on direct observation (a reliance also present, as we shall see, in works that claim to be the reports of travelers themselves) but also to demonstrate the interconnectedness of past and present, of textual representation and direct experience, of geographic fact and geographic fiction within early modern culture. Watreman, the "liberall feaster," takes us on travels with him, imagining ourselves "ledde on [his] hande from countrey to countrey." We become travelers ourselves, engaged in a fictional, fantasy-laden voyage with Watreman who, as Boemus's translator, is placed at an additional remove from the geographic and ethnographic material of the text. The various early modern, medieval, and classical reports become more tightly interwoven into a seamless fabric—or a mind-boggling tangle—which has a great impact on the ways in which sixteenth-century England interpreted references to geographical locations in prose narratives with varying claims to historicity. The importance of trying to separate the strands of this tangle is suggested by comments such as those in Richard Willes's preface to Richard Eden's *History of Travayl* (1577). Willes asks, "Of late who taketh not uppon him to discourse of the whole worlde and eche province thereof particulerly[?]" (fol. Ii^r–ii^v).[7] Moreover, the complicated generic qualities that travel reports embodied were also addressed during the period. Philip Jones's translation of Albertus Meierus's *Certaine briefe and speciall instructions for gentlemen, merchants, students . . . marriners, &c. Employed in seruice abrode, or anie way occasioned to conuerse in the kingdomes, and gouernments of forren Princes* (1589) emphasizes in its dedication the need for travelers to skill themselves in how to make sense of what they experience during their travels: how, in short, to translate experience into an intelligible narrative so that they will not seem "like the foolish youth, that would needs prove a Latinist without his grammar" but who instead "after his ranginges and peregrinations, shall retire him selfe a man of skill."[8] The popularity of such narratives and their factual ambiguity make them of particular importance for early modern prose fiction because of its own varied and tenuous claims to historicity and exemplarity. As factual reports obscure their fictionality, so too do fictional narratives claim factual, historical origins. The generic complexity of such texts creates a complicated reading experience for early modern readers and an even more complicated reading experience for twenty-first-century readers more accustomed to assigning texts to clear discursive categories. The complexity of this reading experience seems aptly echoed in Bhabha's description of his own attempt to discuss the "locality of culture":

> This locality is more *around* temporality than *about* historicity: a form of living that is more complex than "community"; more symbolic than "society"; more connotative than "country"; less patriotic than *patrie;* more rhetorical than the reason of State; more mythological than ideology; less homogeneous than hegemony; less centred than the citizen; more collective than "the subject"; more psychic than civility; more hybrid in the articulation of cultural differences and identifications than can be represented in any hierarchical or binary structuring of social antagonism. (140)

The complexity of this experience for early modern readers makes it extremely difficult for us to recover, even by analogies that can only hint at the difficulties of interpretation and cultural significance that these texts create. We might think, for example, of the clash between the views of Baghdad held by average U.S. citizens raised before the 1990s and those created by subsequent world events: images of Ali Baba and Scheherazade become intertwined with those of scud missiles. For our children raised with the ubiquity of Disney, the narratives of Aladdin and Jasmine become blended together with reports of the life of women under the Taliban in Afghanistan or under the current Saudi government. Eighteenth- and nineteenth-century American captivity narratives might also provide an analogy for these experiences. In these texts, the personal experiences of the narrator become intertwined with ethnographic description (again based on both received material and direct observation) of the captor's culture so that the representation of the culture itself becomes fictionalized.[9]

The intertwining of factual and fictional material within the period's travel and ethnographic discourse may be well illustrated by Thomas Coryate's *Greetings from the Court of the Great Mogul* (1616), which claims to be a letter sent back to England describing Coryate's adventures and observations while in Asmere in East India. Nonetheless, Coryate informs us that the Mogul "keepeth abundance of wilde beasts, & that of diuers sorts, as Lyons, Elephants. Leopards, Beares, Antlops, Vnicornes; whereof two I

Fig. 1. Thomas Coryate, *Greetings from the Court of the Great Mogul* (1616), 24. Reproduced by permission of the Beinecke Rare Book and Manuscript Library, Yale University.

haue seene at his Court, the strangest beasts of the world; they were brought hither out of the Countrie of *Bengala*" (24–25). A woodcut of a unicorn is included, presumably to help concretize his written report (fig. 1).[10]

In addition, the title page of the text also includes a woodcut of a man (presumably Coryate) riding an elephant that has distinctly horselike rear legs—the image, in other words, for all its claims to documentary accuracy, simultaneously fictionalizes Coryate's experience. It domesticates and reduces the Indian elephant to little more than a large, exotic horse, providing a visual image that, as we shall see later in this chapter, participates in the colonialist and didactic motives of early modern ethnography (fig. 2).

Reports of the New World, like those of Coryate and Watreman, are also subject to the distortions of traditional geographical discourse. André Thevet's *Les Singularites de la France Antartique* (1557), translated into English in 1568 as *The New Found Worlde, or Antarticke*,[11] claims to be a report of Thevet's trip to South America. In his "An Admonition to the Reader," in fact, Thevet claims that his work will describe New World plants and animals "which are cleane contrarie to the setting forth of our Cosmographers and Anciente writers, who for because that they haue not sene the places, and for the smal experience and knowledge that they had, did greatly erre"

Thomas Coryate,

TRAVAILER

For the English wits, and the good of this Kingdom:

To all his inferiour Countreymen, Greeting: Espe-
cially to the *Sirenicall Gentlemen*, *that meet the first Friday of euerie*
Moneth, at the Mermaide in Breadstreet. From the Court of
the great *Mogul*, *resident at the Towne of* Asmere, *in the Easterne*
India.

Printed by W. Iaggard, and Henry Fetherston.
1616.

Fig. 2. Coryate, *Greeting from the Court of the Great Mogul* (1616), title page. Reproduced
by permission of the Beinecke Rare Book and Manuscript Library, Yale University.

(unpag.), yet it combines details of his observations with material, as Frank Lestringant has noted, from Vespucci;[12] it also includes material that at least one of Thevet's contemporaries scornfully dismissed as "completely false."[13]

Other forms of geographical texts were also subject to this complex intermingling of fact and fiction. William Cuningham's *The Cosmographical Glasse conteinyng the pleasant Principles of Cosmographie, Geographie, Hydrographie, or Nauigation* (1559), which describes for travelers such skills as how to determine longitudes and latitudes and how to triangulate distances, explains the construction of the text's first part: "And that the præceptes myghte seme the more facile & plaine, I haue reduced it into the forme of a Dialogue: the names of the personages in dede fained, but yet most aptly seruing our institutio[n]" (sig. A.vi^r–v). The factual information, he feels, must be presented more obliquely, through fictional characters. Cosmology and fiction become blended in a desire to create a pleasing text. This textual pull toward the dramatized fictionality of the dialogue, of course, emerges from a long Platonic tradition, but it exists in simultaneous juxtaposition with a drive toward scientific and historical accuracy through a careful attempt to define its terms, both verbally and pictorially.[14] Early on Cuningham has the teacher Philonicus provide Spoudaeus with definitions of cosmography, geography, and chorography. Although Spoudaeus acknowledges that "by your wordes, I haue receued more commoditie at this present, then by all my readyng touching the true diference of these three names," he still requests visual images to supplement each term, because "thinges sene haue longer impresion then only harde" (fol. 7). Philonicus responds by providing three illustrations, demonstrating cosmography's focus on the scientific and the global, geography's focus on land formations, and chorography's focus on very detailed localized mapping.[15] And yet, of course, the included woodcut defining geography contains representations of the four personified winds, linking it to the fanciful and fictional tradition of traveler's reports much more overtly than the scientifically constructed globe or the meticulously labeled chorographical map of the city of Norwich (figs. 3–6).

The discursive complexities of Cuningham's text are amplified as well by the poetic epigraph that appears on the title page:

In this Glasse if you will beholde
   The Sterry Skie, and Yearth so wide,
  The Seas also, with windes so colde,

Fig. 3. William Cuningham, *The Cosmographical Glasse* (1559), title page. Reproduced by permission of the Bodleian Library, University of Oxford.

Fig. 4. Cuningham, *The Cosmographical Glasse* (1559), fol. 7. Reproduced by permission of the Bodleian Library, University of Oxford.

> Yea and thy selfe all these to guide:
> What this Type meane first learne a right,
> So shall the[e] gayne thy trauaill quight.

In these lines are combined the drive of the "new" geography to present the world as it may be observed, and the "old" geography's drive toward reliance on authorities and tradition. The "Glasse" that Cuningham will present will show the reader both the geographic and astronomical realities of the world and a symbolic or allegorical "Type" that will permit the gainful completion of his or her "trauaill." The ambiguities that the lines create are plentiful: Is the "gaine" spiritual or economic? Does "trauaill" refer to actual travel? To the work of learning the geographic and navigational

Fig. 5. Cuningham, *The Cosmographical Glasse* (1559), fol. 8. Reproduced by permission of the Bodleian Library, University of Oxford.

principles within the book? To gaining discursive, colonizing control over distant parts of the world?[16] To the "travaill" of a Christian's life on earth? The factual knowledge of the text will not remain separate from its metaphorical implications. (The combination of historical and allegorical figures—Polibius, Strabo, Astronomia, Arithmetica, etc.—that rim the page provides a visual representation of this interweaving as well.)

Cuningham's use of the image of the "glasse" implies that interpenetration as well. The image of the mirror or glasse was very common during the period; but although it could be used as Hamlet's "mirror up to nature, to show virtue her own feature, scorn her own image, and the very age and body of the time his form and pressure" (3.2.20–22), the imperfections in even the high quality Venetian glass mirrors popular in England during the period caused glasses and mirrors to be linked to distortion and the unreliability of the senses as well.[17] The "glasse" that Cuningham provides for his readers simultaneously presents the scientific reality of the sky, earth, and seas, but it presents an unreliable representation of them as well. Margaret Cavendish, writing just over one hundred years later, calls into question the usefulness of scientific glasses directly in *The Description of a New World Called the Blazing World* (1666), in which scientists who rely on telescopes and microscopes are ridiculed by the Empress for the ways in which their instruments distort their senses: "Nature has made your sense and reason more regular than art has your glasses, for they are mere deluders and will never lead you to the knowledge of truth." The scientists respond, "We take more delight in artificial delusions than in natural truths."[18] Cuningham's image of the "glasse" is an extremely useful one, for it suggests the impossibility of detangling sensory experience of nature from "artificial delusions," of separating fact from fiction. And the link that Cuningham makes between the use of the "glasse" and the reader's "trauaill" further complicates our understanding of the scope of the revelations and distortions to which the reader will be subject: they will range from the local level of the narrow educational project of the book's geographic content to the self-understanding and spiritual edification created by trying to understand more fully his or her place in the macrocosm.

The seamless melding of observation and distortion that Cuningham's text so vividly reflects can be further demonstrated by T. Washington's translation of *The Nauigations, Peregrinations, and Voyages, made into Turkie by Nicholas de Nicholay Daulphinois, Lord of Arfeiule, Chamberlaine and Geographer ordinarie to the King of Fraunce: conteining sundry singularities which the Author hath there seene and obserued* (1585). Not only is it a fairly detailed text that describes a wide range of geographical locations and a number of peoples, but it also contains fifty-six woodcuts, not of fanciful beasts or of rough maps, but of individuals who represent the various locations de Nicholay describes. De Nicholay's text is divided into four books. The first provides a detailed discussion of the travels of the Lord of Aramont, French ambassador to Constantinople, and his party. Individual chapters describe specific places—most notably Algiers, Malta, and Tripoli. They also document certain adventures that befell the European travelers, such as their involvement in the protection of an escaped Christian slave while in Algiers, and

Overleaf: Fig. 6. Cuningham, *The Cosmographical Glasse* (1559), foldout following fol. 8. Reproduced by permission of the Bodleian Library, University of Oxford.

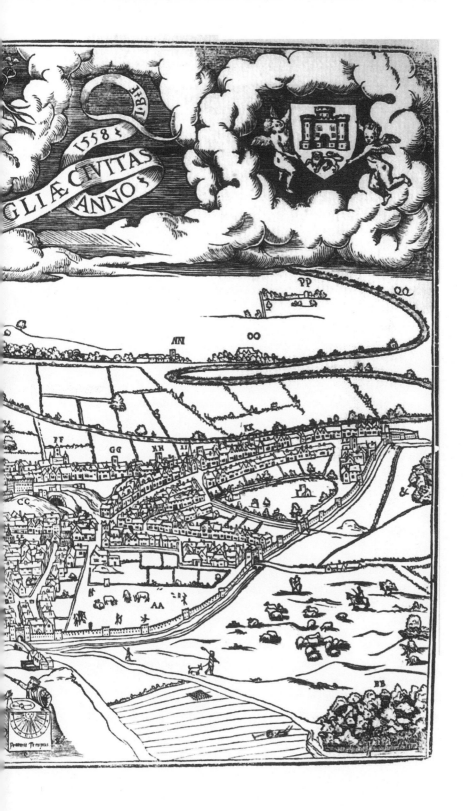

their visit to a bazaar at which Christian slaves are sold. The second book also contains occasional references to the specifics of the Europeans' travels, but a greater percentage of this book is devoted to reporting on the sights purportedly observed by the author, such as Venus's island of "Citheree or Cerigo,"[19] Gallipoli, Mytilene, Constantinople, the seraglio of the Great Turk, and Turkish baths. The third and fourth books shift to more typical ethnographic discussions, defining for readers various kinds of individuals subject to the Turk,[20] as well as similar descriptive material about Persia and Arabia. These later portions of the work lack any pretense to including any firsthand material from de Nicholay's voyage itself. In fact, de Nicholay begins the final section of his work as follows:

> Xenophon in his first booke of Cyropedie, which is to saye, of the life and institution of Cyrus, speaking of the auncient custome of the Persians, sayth that they had a certayne great place called the place of libertie, whereas was the Pallace royall, and other houses publike, and that the same place was deuided into foure quarters. (sig. 113^v)

This discussion of ancient Persian customs, in other words, is based on Xenophon's fictionalized history. It is followed by discussions of Arabian customs and peoples and of people dwelling in Constantinople and Greece. The work concludes twice, as it were, with a final discussion of the terrible subjection of Greeks to "miscreated Mahometists," the result (we are told) of "the righteous iudgements of GOD towards the misbeleeuing, and those that abuse his gracious gifts" (sig. 160^r), and with a caption that serves to introduce three final woodcuts:

> I haue before liuely set forth the figure of a woman of Lacedemonia, to wit, of those which vpon the high waies neere vnto the villages do sell bread vnto the passers by, and hereafter I doe represent vnto you, the Gentleman and the Merchant of Graecia, and the Gentlemans hat must be blacke, as that of the Albanoys, and the tulbant of the merchant must be skie coloured, yee haue also here the portraite of a woman of the countrey in Graecia. (sig. 160^v)

This second conclusion asserts a truth claim based on observational accuracy not generally demonstrated by the language of the text. Typically the woodcuts are not introduced, but when they are, they, like the example just provided, attempt to counterbalance appeals to Xenophon with representational accuracy.

The verbal accounts of the locations de Nicholay's *Navigations* describes—especially after the first two books—are largely free from any sense that the writer's direct observations were permitted to obscure the truths about the cultures that could be culled from earlier sources—they come from Xenophon or Strabo. Similar accounts may be read in *The Fardle of Facions* or Thomas Floyd's *The Picture of a Perfit Common wealth* (1600), but de Nicholay's illustrations are perceived, at least in some instances, as historically accurate. They merit discussion by a first-person voice that uses brief narratives about his own experiences to authorize their claims to verisimilitude. If we as readers gain any sense that the author did actually base his text on his own contact with the cultures he describes, we do so on the basis of the authorial voice that describes the illustrations. The fictionalizing this authorial voice creates is further supported by the woodcuts themselves, which, even as they claim to represent cultural difference, homogenize those differences and turn all figures—Turks, Moors, and Jews—into Europeans. It is a strategy seen in representations of New World figures as well (for example, the well-known de Bry engravings that accompanied the 1590 edition of Thomas Harriot's *A Briefe and True Report of the New Found Land of Virginia*). Their apparel marks the figures as somewhat fantastic, but the attention given to detail suggests that we are to see their clothing as being accurately represented. Colonization is fictionalization. We should understand these woodcuts as part of a strategy by which national identity, to quote Bhabha, may be seen as "a form of social and textual affiliation" (140).

Hodgen's *Early Anthropology in the Sixteenth and Seventeenth Centuries* provides a still useful overview of the nature of ethnographical texts produced during the period and their general unwillingness to rely on direct observation, even when they claim to do so.[21] Moreover, she notes a link between the ethnographic literature and the fictional texts that speaks, I think, to the heart of the argument that I make in this study. In her discussion of Herodotus, whose *Histories* were transmitted to the early modern period most typically in adulterated translated abridgements and epitomes, Hodgen acknowledges that one of Herodotus's descriptive techniques consisted of "the artful insertion of a tale intended to divert the reader, or a dramatic episode to make the historical narrative move."[22] This trait becomes common to the early modern analyst of foreign cultures, and when narratives become inserted into the description of places and customs, the line between fact and fiction becomes even fuzzier. Hodgen herself demonstrates the permeability of the boundary between ethnographic text and fiction, citing Rabelais's *Gargantua* (1534) and *Pantagruel* (1532) as texts that show evidence of the influence of the fantastic elements found in medieval cosmography at the same time that they show contempt for such ungrounded claims about distant cultures. She discusses Pantagruel's encounters with "a diminutive, monstrous, misshapen old Fellow, call'd Hear-say; his Mouth was slit up to his Ears, and in it were seven Tongues, each of them cleft into seven parts." Among the crowd listening to the babble emerging from this enormous mouth are "Herodotus, Pliny, Solinus, Berosus, Philostratus, Pomponius Mela, Strabo, and God knows how many other Antiquaries." Marco Polo is also there.[23] The fictional culture of the period seems, in other words, to be simultaneously rejecting the legendary, fantastic ethnographic tales as well as using them. Julia Kristeva, linking Rabelais's text to sixteenth-century French ethnographic works, observes that such discourse "had difficulty freeing itself from the phantasmal bent" of earlier observers "without falling into another, just as ethnocentrical, reduction that amounted to bringing down the foreigners' strangeness to the same universal logic that Western tradition had brought to the fore" (114). This universalizing tendency might well be termed a fictionalizing one as well: the universal is a fiction. If we can't be sure that the authorities are trustworthy, what difference can we confidently claim between the ethnography of Boemus and the satire of Rabelais? We might provide a similar example from George Whetstone's *The English Myrror* (1586), which, in describing the evils of envy, provides stories from the history of the Holy Roman Empire, the fourteenth-century conflict between the Guelphs and the Gibellines, the New Testament, and the Ottoman Empire. And when Whetstone begins using the following strategy (taken from his chapter on an example of Genovese court intrigue), which parallels opening strategies for early modern novellas, how are we to distinguish between fiction and culturally didactic prose?

> Among all Estates and professions of men, enuy is principally entertained among Courtiers, where euery many laboureth to woorke his fellowes disgrace, and aboue all enuieth his prosperitie, which haue bene the cause of many quarrels, and often times of ciuil commotion, of which there cannot be a more rare and profitable example of admonition, then this which followeth.

At what time the *Genowaies* were Lordes of certaine Cities of the *Leuant*, in the yeere *1380*, It happeneth that . . . (sig. E.ii.)[24]

Storytelling is unavoidable, whether the narratives are factual or fictional. Every story is a travel story; every travel story is a story.

Didacticism, Colonialism, and Fiction

Not only are fiction and ethnography linked by their use of narrative, but the expressed didactic goals of the two genres are also typically very similar, exemplifying what Arthur F. Kinney has called "situational poetics." Their specific rhetorical shape arises from the cultural needs and expectations of both the writers and readers of early modern English culture.[25] Not only do both kinds of texts often enunciate a desire to educate their readers about places and customs with which they have no immediate contact, but they also express moral goals. Robert Allott, in the epistle to the readers that prefaces his *Wits Theater of the Little World* (1599), explains that the "profit that ariseth by reading these epitomized histories [which his work contains] is, to aemulate that which thou likest in others, and to make right vse of their examples" (sig. A.iii^v). Sir Walter Raleigh constructs his *History of the World* (1614), at least in large part, to provide his contemporaries with an instructive demonstration of God's just punishment for sinful behavior: "How Kings and Kingdoms have flourished and fallen; and for what virtue and piety God made prosperous; and for what vice and deformity he made wretched."[26] George Sandys writes that his *A Relation of a Iourney begun An: Dom: 1610. Fovre Bookes Containing a description of the Turkish Empire, of Ægypt, of the Holy Land, of the Remote parts of Italy, and Ilands adioyning,* because it documents the decay into which lands controlled by the Ottoman Empire have fallen, will be seen as providing "threatening instructions" for "the rest of the world."[27] Earlier writers also pronounced moralizing, didactic goals for their works. Watreman's translation of Boemus, for example, explains that many cultures have fallen away from Christianity and become subject to Ottoman control; moreover, Christian unity has been destroyed. The result of this rampant ungodliness is the variety of customs and traditions that he describes in his text (sig. A.vi^v). The moral didacticism in which these texts are engaged is often as clear as their ethnographic, geographic, and historical didacticism. Even when the moralizing element is less clear, it is often alluded to. Thevet merely observes in his "A Preface to the Reader" that God has "put al things in [mankind's?] subiectio[n], that is contained vnder the scope or circuite of the Firmament, to the ende that he might know asmuch as to him was necessary for to attaine to the soueraigne gift" (sig. A.iii.). Robert Coverte, in his *A True and Almost Incredible Report of an Englishman* (1612), tells his readers that "I should prooue ingratefull to my preseruer, not to let the world know his miraculous power."[28] Richard Hakluyt combines his moralizing with nationalism so completely that he has been called "first and foremost a propagandist for long-distance trade and colonization."[29] This combination is often implicit because England is often held up by these texts as praiseworthy for its morality: were it not a superior nation, God would not favor it so. In the dedicatory epistle to Sir Francis Walsingham of the 1589 edition, Hakluyt describes the moment when his uncle introduced him to maps and cosmography. After describing to Hakluyt various cultures and their economic products, his uncle guides him to Psalm 107:23–24, where he reads "that they which go down to the sea in ships, and occupy the great waters, they see the works of the Lord and his wonders in the deep" (31). He couples this belief in the religious value of his project with a desire to describe the adventures of English explorers in a fashion that would bring "the just commendation which our nation does indeed deserve" (33).[30] William Lithgow begins his *Discourse of a Peregrination in Europe, Asia and Affricke* (1614) with no moralizing claim, merely acknowledging that "the nature of man, by an inward inclination, is always inquisitiue of forraine news; yea, and much more affecteth the sight and knowledge of strange and vnfrequented kingdomes, such is the instinct of his natural affection" (sig. B.i), but he uses his discussion of his travels through Italy to describe his disgust for Roman Catholicism.[31]

Hakluyt's successor, Samuel Purchas, whose *Hakluytus Posthumous or Purchas His Pilgrimes* (1624–25) was based on an expanded collection of documents compiled by Hakluyt (which ultimately became more popular than Hakluyt's works), also had a clearly didactic goal, as did his earlier *Purchas His Pilgrimage or Relations of the World and the Religions Obserued in Al Ages and Places Discouered, from the Creation to the Present* (1613), which described the world's religions to show "the vnnaturalness of Faction and Atheisme" (*Pilgrimage*, ded., unpag.).[32] *Purchas His Pilgrimes*, making its colonizing goals clear, explains in its dedication that it will describe how "English inheritance" is dispersed throughout the world by the travelers whose reports "amply relat[e]" the glories of the "English name and nation" (*Pilgrimes*, ded., unpag.). The didacticism, moreover, is transactional and reciprocal—the reports of the travelers both influence the foreign cultures even as they bring home information about them. Purchas, creating what Gillies calls a "Gothic romance" (157) identifies himself as a "poor Zelote" of both England and the king who, like Robert Greene in his preface to *A Notable Discovery of Cozenage* (1591), is quite willing to admit that he has not traveled to those places over which he asserts discursive control (20:130), but he anticipates the role of the travelers whose reports he presents as breeding "New Britaines" in the New World (20:132). Travel reports have an explicit didactic, colonizing aim, one that only gradually becomes separable from the goals of prose fiction.

Raphael Holinshed's *Chronicles of England, Scotland, and Ireland* (1577–87), like Hakluyt's and Purchas's texts, also helps to create a national identity for England, but by turning the techniques of travel narrative inward.[33] Focusing on a kind of internal analysis and appropriation in addition to providing regnal histories of England's rulers, its three folio volumes provide such information as geographical descriptions of England, Wales, Scotland, and Ireland; discussions of their economic products; lists of distances between principle cities; and a list of the number of individuals sent by various cities and towns to Parliament. Its chorographical dimension places it among the texts that Helgerson argues participated in the early modern shift from seeing England as "a system of rule" to a place.[34] Holinshed's dedicatory epistle to Sir William Brooke is interesting for the way in which it contextualizes the material that he presents. Holinshed explains that he was pressured by friends to undertake the project, that the *Chronicles* are the product of his piecing together the works of others—notably John Stowe, Richard Stanyhurst, and Edward Campion,[35] and that he has "neuer trauelled 40. miles foorthright and at one iourney in all my life" (I:vii) except to travel from Kent to London, Cambridge, and Oxford. Like the writers we have already discussed, Holinshed sees actual contact with the locations he will describe as unnecessary. (Robert Greene's claim to have rounded the world "not with travel, yet with experience" might be made by Holinshed as well.) He sees himself as the first to undertake to write the history of Britain, a task that should appeal, he hopes, to the "learned and godlie"[36] (I:viii) who will profit from the difficult task Holinshed has undertaken. The role of Holinshed's *Chronicles* in establishing English nationhood is made more explicit by a letter to "The Readers Studious in Histories" by Abraham

Fleming that precedes the *Chronicles'* History of England, wherein the readers are told that the work of a historian is difficult: "It is a toile without head or taile euen for extraordinarie wits, to correct the accounts of former ages so many hundred yeares receiued, out of uncerteinties to raise certeinties, and to reconcile writers dissenting in opinion and report" (I:426). Although Fleming acknowledges the difficulty of the project, he seems to hold out this ideal—of producing a unified, authoritative document that will report objectively the past experience of England. Holinshed's text, in other words, through its lists of geographical features of the islands, characteristics of the inhabitants, identification of roads, and distances between towns, as well as its descriptions of past events, aims to produce a single documentary Britain: it desires to create a national identity that will be based on fact—it will correct former narratives and "raise certeinties" where no unified narrative has previously existed.[37] In attempting to unify all its geographic, economic, and political activities into one massive book, Holinshed hopes to create a unity out of a diversity of cultures and to provide the British Isles with a clear geographical identity. To create such an identity is, of course, to create a fiction, but such a fiction would have a powerful didactic dimension, unifying England, Scotland, Wales, and Ireland by giving them a common narrative, a common story of their past and their purpose. Moreover, the variety of material that Holinshed includes acts to "empower readers of all sorts" by providing them with the information to make their own decisions.[38] It provides them with a "glasse" through which they may construct their own national identity, permitting them to imaginatively construct England as a de Certeauian "space" that produces a more totalizing fiction of their culture and their place within it.[39]

These travel and historical texts have their fictional analogues: prose fictions also claim to contain representational accuracy of foreign cultures and to see didactic, ethnographic value in such narratives. George Gascoigne's *Hundreth Sundie Flowres* (1573), for instance, suggests historical veracity by inserting the poems and letters into the narrative of *The Adventures of Master FJ* and hiding, by initials, all the identities of the parties involved in what he claims is a true story. In addition, its didactic intent is clear: "The well-minded man may reap some commodity out of the most frivolous works that are written" (Printer to the reader). Thomas Lodge's *Rosalind* (1590) also provides a useful example of the intermingling of fiction and the authority of ethnography. In the prefatory epistle to Lord Hunsdon, Lodge writes:

Having with Captain Clarke made a voyage to the islands of Terceras and the Canaries, to beguile the time with labor I writ this book, rough—as hatched in the storms of the ocean—and feathered in the surges of many perilous seas. (93)

And in the letter to the gentlemen readers:

To be brief, Gentlemen, room for a soldier and a sailor that gives you the fruits of his labors that he wrought in the ocean, when every line was wet with a surge and every humorous passion counterchecked with a storm . . . I fetched it as far as the islands of Terceras, and therefore read it, censure it with favor, and farewell. (95)

Further adding to the geographic cachet of the text, of course, is its full title: *Rosalind: Euphues' Golden Legacy Found after His Death in His Cell at Silexedra,* referring to the location in which Lyly leaves his title character at the end of *Euphues and his England;* in terms of didacticism, the text alludes in its prefaces mostly to the value of the eloquence of the work, and its final paragraph summarizes the instructive purpose of the text, that children should obey their fathers. Robert Greene's cony-catching pamphlets might also be appropriate in this context because, although they don't claim to describe the traditions or geography of foreign countries and cultures, they do provide, like Holinshed's *Chronicles,* a kind of ethnographic description of part of England's cultural landscape, the criminal classes of London. See, for instance, the letter that prefaces his *A Notable Discovery of Cozenage:*

To be brief, Gentlemen, I have seen the world and rounded it; though not with travel yet with experience. . . . I have smiled with the Italian and worn the viper's head in my hand, and yet stopped his venom. I have eaten Spanish *Myrabalans,* and yet am nothing the more metamorphosed. France, Germany, Poland, Denmark: I know them all, yet not affected to any in the form of my life. . . . Yet in all these Counties where I have travelled, I have not seen more excess of vanity than we Englishmen practice through our vainglory. (163)

The text is, like many of Greene's texts, typically ambiguous—has he traveled or hasn't he? The answer does not really matter. English vainglory results in the culture's contentment at failing to punish the cony-catchers that his work goes on to describe. A more significant and overt mingling of fact and fiction might be provided by Nashe's *The Unfortunate Traveller,* especially in its early sections, which create an air of factuality through its references to Henry VIII and other historical figures, a strategy also employed by Thomas Deloney in his novels. John Lyly's romances also contain an ethnographic strategy, although not through reference to historical figures but rather through its style: the employing of analogies from natural history marks the text as being as educational as its plot is moralizing.[40]

A final example might be provided of the links between fiction and geographic texts that I am making here. George Sandys, in his *A Relation of a Iourney begun An. Dom. 1610* (1615), includes in his general description of Egypt and its culture a discussion of hieroglyphs and includes a woodcut of one (fig. 7) "said to be pourtrayed within the porch of *Minerua's* Temple in the Citie of *Sai*" and based on a description included in Plutarch's *Isis and Osiris.*[41] The image is interpreted in Sandys's text. The "Infant" (top left) represents "those that enter the world," the old man "those that go out of it"; the falcon represents God, the fish hatred ("because they hated fish that bred in the Sea"), and the "Riuer-horse" "murder, impudence, violence, and iniustice." Read as a sentence, the hieroglyph means, according to Sandys: *"O you that enter the world, and go out of it; God hateth iniustice"* (105). One might wonder to which God the text refers. It seems that the Egyptian hieroglyph found in a Greek temple refers to a Judeo-Christian God—a clear instance of the traveler translating the foreign Other into the humanist ideology of his own culture, erasing cultural difference. The European-style rendering of the images themselves also confirms that we are getting not a "true" representation of hieroglyphic images but a European interpretation of them. Interpreting these elements of the text—the woodcut and Sandys's interpretation of it—the reader receives an unqualified report of a facet of Egyptian culture that claims to represent it honestly, but in so doing elides its own cultural distortions, the ways in which it is fictionalizing Egyptian culture. However, the reader is not left to settle for this interpretation of the image and Sandys's text. A marginal gloss alongside the image reads: "In this Hippopo-som the cutter chose rather to follow than re-forme an error" (105). How does this effect the reader's perception of the image and Sandys's analysis of it? To what error does the gloss refer? What is the effect of this additional editorial voice? The reader is left aware that something is amiss but not sure what. The image is left with precarious authority—some-

Fig. 7. George Sandys, *A Relation of a Iourney begun An. Dom. 1610* (1615), 105. Reproduced by permission of the Bodleian Library, University of Oxford.

thing about it is wrong, presumably with the horse image, but what? The reader is asked simultaneously to accept Sandys's account as factual and to recognize that it contains an error that renders it a misrepresentation, a fictionalized account of the cultural artifact it claims to represent. And this misrepresentation is what the culture often seemed to prefer to factual accounts. Jonathan Haynes, in *The Humanist as Traveler,* explains that Sandys and many of his contemporaries tended to rely more heavily on classical descriptions of Egyptian artifacts than on the few examples available to them. The engraver in this instance could have used the statuettes that Sandys brought back from Egypt as stylistic models, but instead chose to render Plutarch's images in a traditional European manner, just as Sandys had relied on his classical source rather than his own observation (86). The report of a contemporary actual trip—the authenticity of which is even attested to on the title page by the inclusion of the date of the author's departure from England—becomes fictionalized and classicized, visual images notwithstanding. The hieroglyph, like Coryate's unicorn, is illustrated, as if to assure readers of its factual nature, but the documentary nature of the visual image is undermined by the fictional nature of the image itself. In Sandys's case, the editor, who elsewhere provides translations for Latin passages and identifications of sources and historical individuals, is uncomfortable with the fiction, with the "error," though he leaves the reader uncertain as to what aspect of the error disturbs him.

Fact and fiction again blur, space and place do as well (to return to de Certeau). What begins as a rather conventional cribbing from Plutarch is situated within a discussion of an individual's specific travel experiences (the passage is framed between discussion of his voyage from Rhodes to Egypt [92] and direct references to his own experiences ["Diuers of the women haue I seene" [109]) and is qualified by the editor's announcing his decision to leave in the "error" that the hieroglyph contains. The reader then is asked to create a very complex location within his or her mind, a "space" simultaneously able to regard Sandys's account as factual observation, conventional wisdom, and fictional representation. It is just such spaces that the fiction of the period also asks its readers to create.

2

The Gendered and Geographic "Glasses" of the English Novella

Significant too is that the creation of spaces within ethnographic and fictional texts often simultaneously enables the creation of definitions of gender identity and acceptable sexual practice. Geographic and gender education go hand in hand. Without wanting to overstate claims for the period's prose fiction, I suggest that the discourses of cultural and racial difference, national identity, gender construction, and sexuality all become mutually active within these texts, creating occasions for cross-fertilization and cross-definition not possible in other early modern genres. As Timothy Hampton writes about the use of factual material, in particular the use of historical figures within fictional discourses, "One of the normalizing functions of exemplarity is to offer images of coherent, ideologically marked subjects whose bodies and histories function in harmony."[1] These images are mutually didactic.

The Boccaccian collections of short fiction that flourished during the sixteenth century provide a useful entry into a discussion of this confluence precisely because of their similarity to the ethnographic materials; in other words, because of their claim to exemplarity. Such claims to historicity—as are frequently found in the opening sentences of tales that define the location and the monarch governing the story's setting—provide ample opportunity to examine the implications of geographic Otherness and cultural difference on fictional narrative. These collections of novellas, including as they do a number of narratives representing a number of perspectives, provided writers with a means to make tentative attempts at representing the cultures they described impartially even as they reinforced the stereotypes they superficially seem to be rejecting. The novella collections also provide a useful means of examining the representation of cultural difference because they are, in general, themselves so fully infused with cultural multiplicity and are, as Marcel Tetel observes, texts that easily lent themselves to combining authorial originality with the drive to imitate.[2] Because most of the best-known collections—Fenton's *Certaine Tragicall Discourses*, Painter's *Palace of Pleasure*, Pettie's *Petite Palace*—are based on continental sources, they carry with them interpretations of, in particular, Eastern cultures that may represent a more broadly European perception of the cultures to which they allude. In fact, R. W. Maslen has commented that writers such as Painter and Fenton handled their Italian source material "as if it were an expensive and highly dangerous exotic beast which needed to be kept at bay with every editorial control at their disposal."[3] The understanding that the material presented by the collections was "exotic" seems to resonate throughout the collections by writers such as Fenton and Painter, and they anticipate that this understanding will intrigue and educate their readers as well.

In the dedication of his 1566 *Palace of Pleasure* to the Earl of Warwick, William Painter writes that the tales he has collected display

> the uglye shapes of insolence and pride, the deforme figures of incontinencie and rape, the cruell aspectes of spoyle, breach of order, treason, ill lucke and overthrow of states and other persons. . . . [S]ome of these may seeme to intreat of unlawfull love and the foule practises of the same, yet being throughly read and well considered, both old and yonge may learne how to avoyde the ruine, overthrow, inconvenience and displeasure, that lascivious desire and wanton wil doth bring to their suters and pursuers. All which maye render good examples, the best to be followed, and the worst to be avoyded: for which intent and purpose be all things good and bad recited in histories, chronicles and monumentes, by the first authors and elucubrators of the same.[4]

Certainly there is a conventional component to this claim that the stories he is about to present will serve a didactic purpose, but the passage also reveals what is a very substantial concern for the English "elucubrators" (literally, "those who compose by lamplight"), the collectors and translators of novellas in English. As Paul Salzman explains, Painter sees part of the appeal of his tales as a result of "their vividness, their ability to present a scene before the eyes of the reader."[5] Geoffrey Fenton's dedication to Mary Sidney at the beginning of his *Certaine Tragical Discourses* (1567) also asserts a didactic goal.[6] Fenton wants to help correct the ill behavior of his age; he also asserts in this letter that all classes of English society need knowledge of

> worldly thinges . . . [which] can not be gotten but by the assistance of histories, who are the onelye and true tables whereon are drawne in perfecte coollers the vertues and vices of everye condicion of man . . . that excellent treasore and full librarye of all knowledge yeldes us frelye presidentes for all cases that may happen; both for imytacion of the good, detestynge the wycked, avodynge a present mischiefe, and preventynge any evil afore yt fall.[7]

Histories, in other words, are by their very nature instructive. And, as Lorna Hutson demonstrates in *The Usurer's Daughter: Male Friendship and Fictions of Women in Sixteenth-Century England,* Fenton's concern here is with factual military histories as much as it is with the fictional romantic histories he is about to present. She succinctly observes, "It was classical military history which offered the primary conceptual model for fictions of civil courtship."[8] Both histories and fiction provide exempla; both are instructive, although certainly the degree to which they succeed in their ability to function in this role is open to question.[9] Sir Philip Sidney's *Defense of Poetry* could be cited as making a similar point.

The nature of the didactic dimension of these novella collections varies in emphasis once the writers leave their dedications behind and turn to the tales themselves, but that didacticism becomes significantly gendered, as shown by the subject matter and frequent direct addresses to readers.[10] This gendering is not merely the result of a desire to appeal to female readers; it also reflects a desire to fashion and channel male constructions of identity. As Hutson observes:

> The centrality of women to [novella collections] is not, then, necessarily a concession to the tastes of women readers, nor even a concessionary move from the "public" to the "private" sphere. Rather it is that fictions of women, focusing men's narratives of persuasive efficiency, become coextensive with the enterprise of authorship itself as the medium of masculine social advancement. For, as humanism relocated the space of trial for masculine *virtus* from battlefield to text,

so anthologies (rhetorical "gatherings" of poetry and fictional history), appearing in print before men's eyes, became the new place in which men displayed the cerebral equivalent of chivalric prowess, in virtuoso deployments of their skill in probable argument.[11]

These collections demonstrate their authors' cerebral prowess generally within the framework of fictional romantic histories that interrogate the nature of relationships between men and women and the more narrow analysis of the functioning of reason, passion, and definitions of orthodox and transgressive desire. They afford male authors the opportunity to explore strategies for defining, describing, and satisfying heterosexual male desire in ways acceptable to a culture that was seen as increasingly turning from the battlefield to the bedchamber as its site of military confrontation—as can be seen in Barnaby Riche's prefaces to his *Farewell to Militarie Profession* (1581) or even the opening soliloquy of Shakespeare's *Richard III*.

Moreover, this movement from battlefield to bedroom is coexistent with an additional geographic movement.[12] Perhaps simply because "every story is a travel story" (to return to de Certeau) the novellas presented by Painter, Fenton, Pettie, and the others provide their readers with specific links between the construction and containment of desire and the colonizing discourse that so often masks itself as a geographic and ethnographic "glasse."

Cultural Difference, Military Prowess, and Sexual Violence

Although most of the geographic references are to Italian cities and provinces, as should be expected since Italian authors provide the majority of the source material, the novella collections also provide information about non-European, non-Christian cultures. Fenton's *Discourses* provides many instances of this kind of characterization of the East, for example: "a company of effemynate Persians" (II.59); "th'incursions of the blasphemous infidells and ennemies of our religyon" (II.104); "the desperat Persyans" (II.111); "the barbarous disposicion of the Turke, or Moare, or other infidell withoute religion or faith" (II.209–10); and "the most furious and savage beastes that ever bredd in the desertes of Lybia" (II.268). These nuggets of information and innuendo act to stigmatize and place the East under European discursive control. And the importance of this cultural or geographic didactic element, which might be aligned with the "nationalist pedagogy"

Homi Bhabha finds present in the textual production of a culture, is extremely important.[13] Matteo Bandello, writing in a dedicatory epistle contained in his novella collection (1554), one of the most influential Italian anthologies, explores more fully the need for education about geographical difference in general and the threat posed by the East more specifically:

> Again, in worldly matters this age of ours has seen the Turks take all of Syria, and the Sultan defeated with his mercenary crew, Belgrade conquered, Rhodes at war, most of Hungary subjugated, and Vienna in Austria besieged, and great damages done in those countries, with the expectation of worse, to the unspeakable shame of all Christendom, which has by now been reduced to a corner of Europe thanks to the discords which now grow greater every day among Christian princes. Those who ought to stand up against the Turkish might and cruelty have spilled so much Christian blood that it would have been sufficient to recapture the Empire of Constantinople and the Kingdom of Jerusalem. . . . We have seen the Great Shepherd of Rome, a prisoner of the Germans and Spanish, buy his freedom from the Emperor Charles, and Rome cruelly sacked, the churches pillaged, the nuns raped, and all cruelties one can imagine perpetrated, so that the Goths of former times were more merciful. . . . The Emperor and the King of France are now at war and now at truce, and yet one sees no peace agreement. The Venetians have been forced to buy peace from the Turks and to give them part of their land. . . . And certainly we can say that very few ages have seen as sudden changes as we see daily, nor do I know where all these things will end, because it seems to me that we are going from bad to worse and that among the Christians there is more discord than ever.[14]

Bandello's lament focuses on early modern European anxiety about the dissolution or erasure of national and cultural identities, an anxiety that often manifests itself in the kind of brief geographical allusion described earlier and in tales that use the East as an important location. The fear that Bandello enunciates of "going from bad to worse" often translates to the page in terms of the interplay among different places and different cultures, and sexual violence is intimately folded into this set of cultural fears. The raping of nuns merits Bandello's emphasis as a new and particularly heinous form of violence created by the Christian inability to eliminate the threat the Ottoman Empire poses to the West, and this violence crosses both sexual and cultural boundaries—its victims are both women and representatives of Bandello's culture, and their rape is an aggressive military act of cultural annihilation as much as it is a private act of personal, sexual assault. It straddles the boundaries between the arenas of *virtus* Hutson describes.[15]

When Eastern locations are not used in brief allusions within these tales but as locations that figure in the narratives' plots, they are often likely to be linked to qualities that the European male reader fears and that become narratively linked to violence against women: the domination of passion, the erasure of reason, and the fear of male subordination to women. Maslen, in a very cogent discussion of Painter's and Fenton's collections, convincingly argues that Fenton's text is "dominated by fierce and unpredictable women," as is Painter's text—especially in the ten stories Painter adapts from Marguerite de Navarre's *Heptameron*.[16] Although not dwelling on the ethnographic dimensions of these texts, Maslen emphasizes the way in which Painter and Fenton (as well as those individuals who wrote commendatory verses for their volumes) emphasized the strangeness of their texts—in the sense of them as both "innovative" and "foreign."[17] These collections present, in other words, a means of emphasizing both cultural difference and the nature of gender identity—in the novella collections the two are inseparably linked.

One tale in which this link is clearly established is William Painter's tale of Amadour and Florinda (I.53), which is among those he derives from the *Heptameron*. Painter summarizes the tale as presenting "the loue of Amadour and Florinda: wherein be conteined mani sleightes and dissimulations, together with the renowmed chastitie of the said Florinda" (2.129). Florinda's chastity doesn't just resist "mani sleightes and dissimulations," it resists two rape attempts, the second of which is fairly graphically described. The tale charts the progress over several years of the love of Amadour, a valiant Spanish gentleman, for the young, aristocratic Florinda. During the course of the tale, Amadour marries in order to provide a cover for his virtuous passion for Florinda, and he pursues a mistress in order to provide further distraction for those suspicious individuals who think he may love her. She falls in love with one nobleman who loves someone else and then enters into a loveless marriage out of political necessity. Eventually, Amadour, who "through the force of love had lost al reason" (2.142), attempts to rape her. During the first of the attempted rape scenes, we are simply told that "he attempted that which the honor of womanhode doth defend" (2.142) and that he "pursued his purpose so earnestly as he could" (2.142). She, believing he is sick and not ill intentioned, fends him off by calling in the aid of a gentleman in the next room. Subsequently, Florinda remains suspicious of Amadour and in preparation for the second scene of attempted rape, she "tooke up a stone which was within the chapell, and gave her selfe so great a blowe on the face that her mouthe, eyes and nose, were altogether deformed"; she then intentionally "fell downe uppon a great stone" (2.146). This second scene builds on that description of self-violence:

> Florinda sawe his face and eyes so altered, and that the fairest die and colour of the world, was become so red as fier, with his most pleasaunt and amiable loke transformed into horrible hew and furious, and therewithall discried the very hote burning fier to sparkle within his harte and face: and how in that fury with one of his strong fistes he griped her delicate and tender hands: and on the other side shee seeing all her defences to fayle her, and that her feete and handes wer caught in such captivitie as she could neither run away nor yet defend her selfe. (2.146)[18]

She tries to reason with him, but his response is to say, "Since I can get nothing of you but the bare bones and carcase, I will holde them so fast as I can" (2.147). She finally thwarts his attack by crying out for her mother, who had arranged this meeting between the two characters in the first place.

What makes the tale of Amadour and Florinda pertinent to my discussion here is the way in which cultural difference and military prowess frame these scenes of sexual violence.[19] The sexual violence in the scenes just described is self-evident, and its thematic significance is fairly clear. The text makes literal the frequently used Petrarchan metaphor of war as emblematic of the conflict that love creates between reason and passion. One of the goals of this novella seems to be to provide a means by which the struggle between reason and passion may be played out and explored; however, as Marcel Tetel has observed, in Marguerite's version of the tale the military image is used "at a very earthy level." It is reduced to "the conquest of a woman by a man and the incessant confrontations between the two in order to effectuate this conquest."[20] Painter's version operates similarly, although his imagery is not as consistent as hers. Before the first scene of attack, Amadour's profession of love to Florinda and his subsequent behavior had spurred her to jealousy. Upset with her reaction, he decides "to dissemble mine anger" (2.136)[21] and to return to a military life. We are told that he fights with the King of Spain at Perpignan and is ultimately confronted by the troops of the King of Tunis. Their superior strength convinces him that it would be "better to render himself, than to be cause of the losse of so many good souldiours as were under his governmente" (2.139), and so he surrenders and is taken as a prisoner to Tunis. He is imprisoned by the Turks for two years until he is finally permitted to go seek his ransom. This reprieve comes just when we are told that "the king [of Tunis] was minded to offer him the gibbet, or els make him renounce his fayth, for the desire hee had to retaine him still, and to make him a good Turke" (2.140). The second scene of attempted rape is also followed by reference to the non-Christian world, a reference that makes explicit the parallels between sexual peril and cultural dissolution. Amadour is appointed to do battle against the Moors led by the King of Granada. In this battle, Florinda's husband is killed and her brother is wounded. Amadour finds himself surrounded by the enemy. He decides, we are told by the narrator, that

> because he would bee no more taken, as well to verifie his faith towardes God as also his vowe made to his lady, and also considering that if he were prysoner to the kyng of Granado, either hee should cruelly be put to death, or els forced to renounce his faith, he determined not to make his death or taking glorious to his enemies. (2.150)

He makes this decision so that he will not be forced to renounce Christianity; he kisses the "crosse of his sworde" and impales himself on it. Florinda ends the tale by entering a convent and focusing her attentions on "the perfit love of God" (2.150). Interestingly, Painter tries to recoup Amadour's reputation here, just as he had tried to soften Marguerite's tone toward him throughout the tale. In Marguerite's version, the corresponding passage explicitly refers twice to his abuse of Floride, as the female character is there named: "as he had failed to take his lady," his enemies will fail to take him, and "his faith to her he had broken" but his vow to God he would not break (152).

Amadour's initial attempt to suppress his anger at Florinda's jealousy places him in the world of the Turks where he attempts, in Tetel's phrase, to "reassert himself after sentimental defeats" (Tetel 30). There he does not become a victorious warrior; rather, he is captured, resulting in an "immeasurable loss" (as Patricia Frances Cholakian, referring to Marguerite de Navarre's tale, has called it) to his country.[22] He is an exemplary hostage whom the

King of Tunis would like to make "a good Turk." When he returns to Europe, he does not do so in absolute terms. He returns to drum up his ransom, still linked to the non-European world, and he drags that realm with him.[23] His transgression of the bounds of a *serviteur* removes him from full participation within the Christian European world. The violence of the rape scenes is then infused with traces of the non-European Turk, and that world may be said to be implicated in the failure of reason to restrain Amadour's passion. The gross violence to which Amadour succumbs may be read, then, as a sign of his inability to channel his desire in humanistically acceptable ways and of his affiliation with the non-European Other. His decision to kill himself rather than be captured a second time and forced to renounce his faith—and his choosing to do so in a manner also suggestive of rape—makes literal his desperate fear of losing his Christian, "reasonable" identity. This fear had been triggered by Florinda's jealousy, enhanced by his captivity by the Turks, and brought to a crisis by the violence of his attempted rape of her and the later military supremacy of the Turks. That the violence prompted by unrestrained sexual desire results in fear of cultural annihilation is evident in Amadour's language in Marguerite's version even more clearly than Painter's. Just before his suicide, rather than being subjected to the gibbet, in Marguerite's text he chooses self-impalement rather than the impalement that the King of Tunis had planned for him; he chooses to phrase his decision in relation to his earlier actions with Floride ("Even as he had failed to take his lady, so now his enemies would be frustrated in taking him" [152]), so that the loss of cultural identity in the male is equated with sexual violence against both his beloved and himself. In other words, fear of cultural loss becomes played out on the body; it becomes symbolically enacted not only as his failed attempt to take her by force, but also as her violence against herself and his refusal to be taken by force as well. Both characters become the agents of their own objectification and disfigurement.

The objectification of Florinda meets with specific approval in the period itself from George Pettie, who valorizes her behavior as part of his commentary on the tale of Pygmalion, contained in his 1576 *A Petite Palace of Pettie His Pleasure:*

> So may *Florinda* bee a fruitfull example to the feminine sorte, to doe the like, who bearyng sutch fervent affection to fer freinde *Amadour,* that shee helde him more dere then her owne life, that she received more contentacion in the companie of him, then of husband, father, mother,

. . . freinde or whosoever: yet shee was so far of from filthy affection towards him, that shee avoyded, so neare as shee could, all occasions which might draw him into any disordinate desire towardes her. In so mutch, that havyng occasion of privie conference with him in a private place, beefore she came, shee fouly defaced her face, and bruised it with a stoane, that hee might not bee inflamed with the feature thereof, and divers other wayes at divers other times, valiantly withstoode all alarms of lust. Therfore they are no doubt deceived, which thinke that love cannot bee without lust, neither fervent affection without fleshly fancie.[24]

She tries, Pettie asserts, to prevent the creation of "disordinate" desire: she acts to "order" Amadour's desire by becoming violent against herself in order to try to enable Amadour to create a socially acceptable version of his desire. The extremity and severity of the wounds she inflicts upon herself suggest the strength of Amadour's desire and the insufficiency of conventional erotic outlets for it—it is only the military world of aggression against the Turk that provides a culturally sanctioned (if limited) means for the assertion of his *virtus*.

"Barbarous Nations," "Lymytrophall Townes," and Placing the Novella

Geoffrey Fenton's *Certaine Tragicall Discourses* provides a good text from which to draw further examples of the ways in which setting a narrative within a location of geographic and cultural Otherness, particularly that of the non-Christian East, becomes linked to scenes of violence against women, because it is among the earliest collections to import the Italian tales into England. (William Painter's *The Palace of Pleasure*, vol. 1, was published in 1566. Fenton's collection appeared before the second volume of Painter's collection was published in 1567.) The text contains thirteen tales based on Bandello's novellas as they were translated into French by Belleforest. In general, as René Pruvost observed in 1937, Fenton tends to amplify his models greatly, adding more passages of rhetorical grandiloquence, much more moralizing, and more consistent attempts at analysis of his characters than is found in Painter or his sources.[25] This moralizing tone emerges from his desire to authorize his text as didactically significant, as well as from Fenton's patriotic, anti-Italian, and anti-Catholic biases.[26] Maslen argues that Fenton's text (like Painter's) has a nationalistic didactic purpose as well in its appropriation of Continental novella, asserting that "a writer who knew how to report or even to duplicate the subterfuges of Catholic infiltrators might prove himself invaluable to the counter-espionage activities of the Elizabethan state."[27]

Fenton's Discourse 12, "Perillo suffreth muche for the love of Carmosyna, and marienge her in the ende, were both two striken to deathe with a thonderbolte, the firste night of their unfortunat mariage" (II.213), like the tale of Amadour and Florinda, also involves an episode of imprisonment by Turks. Unlike that tale, however, in which contact with the East prompts a loss of reason in the male, which then results in violence against the female and her own violence against herself, here contact with the East empowers the female. In an attempt to earn the approval of Carmosyna's father for their marriage, Perillo joins a merchant voyage to Alexandria that is blown to the Barbary Coast where it is set upon by Moorish pirates (II.225), and he is imprisoned in Tunis "to lyve in extreme miserye under the servile yoke of the barbarous nations" (II.226). Perillo is eventually released and undertakes a second merchant venture (funded by Carmosyna), which earns him enough money to be granted her father's permission to marry her. As in the story of Amadour and Florinda, it is the intervention of the East that facilitates Carmosyna's willingness to aid her beloved: before his capture she tells him she must rely on her parents' will in determining their future. After his imprisonment she is willing to supply him with funds and to plan to find a means to effect his release (although he is released before she is able to implement her plan). There seems to be some element that the "barbarous nations" represent that empowers Carmosyna to control money (since Carmosyna had not funded his initial voyage) and to take an active role in ensuring her union with the man she selects. The East seems to free her to act both economically and sexually. As in the tale of Amadour and Florinda, contact with the East seems to provoke an ability to abandon certain European, Christian conventions. In Marguerite and Painter's tales, it authorizes the destructive releasing of Amadour's passions and subjects Florinda to the dehumanizing violence of them. In Fenton's text, the result of Turkish imprisonment may be even more threatening to an English audience, as it displaces the influence onto the female character in the narrative (as was ultimately the case in the Amadour-Florinda tale), not to victimize her but to authorize her economic independence. Fenton's "Perillo and Carmosyna" differs from the Amadour and Florinda tale in interesting ways: whereas contact with and imprisonment by the Turks prompts Amadour to violence and unrestrained passion, in Fenton's discourse it stimulates the female character to economic and sexual action. It eliminates her passivity and objectification, whereas it prompts Amadour to view Florinda in just such objectifying terms. Regardless of these differences, however, there is an intriguing similarity between the two tales. Carmosyna, like Florinda, is prone to self-violence, and after learning of Perillo's capture, she falls "into suche presente rage that she was redy to use force against herselfe" (2.227) and must be physically restrained.

Fenton's *Discourses* provides further ways in which locating a novella in an Eastern location becomes a kind of touchstone, unleashing threatening behavior in Christian Europeans as well as providing examples of ways in which Eastern allusions present more explicit threats of physical violence against women. Fenton's fourth tale, "An Albanoyse Capteine, being at the poynte to dye, kylled his wyfe, because no man should enjoye her beawtie after his deathe,"[28] begins with the following sentence:

> Duringe the sege and miserable sacke of Modona (a cytye of the Mores, confyning upon the sea Peloponese, not farr from the straite of Ysthmyon, by the whiche the Venetians conveighe theire great traffique and trade of marchandise) Baiazeth, th'emperour of the Turkes, and great grandfather to Sultan Solyman who this daye governeth the state of th'oriente, used so many sortes of inordinat cruelties in the persecution of those wretches whom fate, with extreme force of his warr, had not onlye abandoned from the soyle of their ancient and naturall bode, but also (as people ful of desolation and voide of succour euery ways) forced them to craue harbor of the lymytrophall townes, adjoyning their countrey, to shroude ther weary bodyes, bledinge still with the woundes of their late warre, and overcome besides wth the violence of hungar and cold—ii comon enemies that neuer faile to followe the campe of miserie. (I.165)

From these "lymytrophall townes" the captain flees to Mantua with his wife. The Turkish wars do not figure again in Fenton's tale, but they have established the captain and his wife as exiles, as characters thrust into the events of the narrative by the horrors of war against the Turks. (It is perhaps significant too, in our attempt to explore the ways in which cultural difference and racism function in the text to notice that Modona is called a city of the "Mores"; that is, it is part of the province of Greece formerly known as Morea, but a term that also cannot help but echo with associations of the African Moors. This strategy is also used in another collection we will later consider, William Averell's *A Dyall for Dainty Darlings* [1584].) This opening also serves to remind readers of current political affairs in the region. Baiazeth is the great grandfather of Soliman, the current ruler of "the state of th'oriente," the ruler that Painter—also writing in 1567—had warned his readers about. Had not the Turks disrupted the lives of the tale's central characters, the captain would not have been driven to his murderous actions, for he is driven to suicidal despair by the death of his protector (I.182). In this case, contact with the non-European prompts loss of reason in the male and violent victimization of the female, although not the additional self-violence to which Florinda/Floride had been subjected.

Within the framework of a collection of "histories" that has as part of its stated intention the "avodynge a present mischiefe, and preventynge any evil afore yt fall," the use of the Turkish contact provides a subtle attempt to link violence against women to the need to colonize and destroy the Ottoman Empire. Further didactic moments in the tale are more explicit. The captain's unfortunate wife, for example, hoping to save her own life and comfort her husband, explains to him that

> the scripture . . . forbides us to yelde any debte or dutie at all to suche as be alredie passed out of the worlde, and muche lesse to sacrifyze ourselves for their sakes upon their tombes (accordynge to the supersticious order of the barbarians in olde time, remeinyng at this daye in no lesse use amonge the people of the weste worlde). (I.185)

A marginal gloss at this point informs the readers that we are here learning about "a ceremonie amongst the barbarians to sacrafise themselves uppon the tombes of their deade frendes" (I.185). Slightly later in the text, as the jealous captain is about to stab to death his blameless wife, the narrator informs us that his rage was "far excedinge the savage and brutishe maner of the tiger, lyon, or libarde, bredd in the desertes of Affrike, the common norsse of monsters and creatures cruell without reason" (I.188–89). These two moments in the story differ in degree more than kind. The first is an attempt to teach readers about ancient customs practiced by non-Christians; the second example allows its prejudices to speak more openly. Its goal is not to teach the reader about a custom or part of natural history; its goal is to characterize the savagery of the captain, to dehumanize him and Africa under the guise of didacticism. And these moments occur within a larger framework of Eastern savagery and aggression against which heterosexual male desire becomes figured as requiring violence against women.

An additional Fenton tale also includes the East, although in the form of Turkish pirates, not soldiers. In "Luchyn is Longe in Love wyth a Simple Mayde, whom he woeth and cannot wyn by any passion hee endureth" (II.129),[29] the "simple mayde," Janiquetta is not threatened by physical violence (at either her own hand or that of another), but she is forced to propose prostituting herself as a result of the poverty into which she falls after her husband is captured by Turkish pirates. Explicit references to the East in this tale are few—in addition to learning that her husband is imprisoned in "a towne subject to the Turkishe governmente" (II.159), there is mention of Cleopatra (II.137) and "Orient coullers" (II.153). Nonetheless, the East is a necessary precondition for the events of the tale—it prompts Janiquetta's proposed prostitution as well as Luchyn's sublimation of his desire for her (for he helps her without demanding that she submit herself to him). She is kept from the sexual violence of forced prostitution and Luchyn is praised for his "heroicall vertue" (II.163) at the end of the tale. Moreover, the tale concludes with Janiquetta's husband still imprisoned by the Turks, suggesting that Janiquetta is saved from violence only by isolating her from male desire that has been tainted by the East. She ends the tale chastely and safely, but only by sacrificing a Christian male to the barbarous Eastern Other.

The link between the East and the violent effects of male desire on female characters continues through later novella collections as well. In George Whetstone's *An Heptameron of Ciuill Discourses* (1582), a text combining elements of the Boccaccian collection with courtesy literature,[30] emphasizes even more than Marguerite de Navarre the philosophical discussions about marriage and gender relations that surround the narratives.[31] The best-known narrative in the collection is the tale of Promos and Cassandra, told on the fourth day by the only female character who narrates a story within the text and who does so to demonstrate that men are much more capable of "treacherie" (125) than women. Like many of the tales already considered, the tale is set in Europe but is framed against the East. It begins:

> At what time *Corvinus* the scourge of the *Turkes,* rayned as Kinge of *Bohemia:* for to well governe the free Cities of his Realme, hee sent divers worthy Majestrates. Among the rest, he gave the Lorde *Promos* the Lieutennauntship of *Julio:* who in the beginning of his govern-

ment, purged the Cittie of many ancient vices, and severely punished new offenders. (125)

Diane Shklanka, citing C. T. Prouty, identifies "Julio" as Jula or Gyula in eastern Hungary; it has also been suggested that it may be a reference to Vienna.[32] Although Corvinus is not a Turk, and "Julio" is not an Eastern location in itself, both have Eastern connections: the first because his reputation during the sixteenth century was established not only as a just administrator but also as a defender of the West against the Turks—Painter had called him "the first ["of any Prynce that governed that kingdome"] that was Famous, or feared of the Turks"[33]; the second because it would be on the edge of the territory the Ottomans attempted to conquer.

The plot of the tale is very similar to that of Shakespeare's *Measure for Measure,* except that in Whetstone's prose version the heroine must submit to the rape prompted by Promos's sexual blackmail.[34] After Corvinus has revealed Promos's crime, the lieutenant is married to Cassandra and sentenced to be executed, a punishment that is remitted through Cassandra's pleas and Promos's repentance. The narrator concludes the tale by telling her audience that "from betweene the teethe of daunger, every partie was preserved, and in the ende establyshed in their hartes desire" (137). Again the Eastern frame contextualizes the violent exercising of male desire and power: Corvinus is the "scourge of the Turks." Moreover, the tale is set in Hungary, which was positioned on the edge of mid-sixteenth-century Turkish incursions into Christian Europe. As such, the narrative situates itself as part of the cultural apparatus concerned with staving off threats to its autonomy, its structures, and its values. In other words, the frame of this tale signals that it is treatment such as that given to Cassandra that has been protected by Corvinus's repulsion of the Turks: it emphasizes the abuse of Cassandra as part of the strength of European culture. Whereas the East provided the spur to the violent exercising of desire, in this case the violence has been internalized. The ability of the West to defeat the Turks becomes simultaneously figured as the ability of the West to authorize and validate sexual violence against women. Promos's rape of Cassandra is legitimated by marriage, and all the characters ultimately achieve "their hartes desire" (137).

Significant too is what this tale does to the text as a whole—after it is told no other extended narratives are included within the text until the last day, when the host, Signor Philoxenus, whose name means "friendly to strangers,"[35] inserts a tale about two Ionian lovers whose marriage brings peace to their parents' warring cities, a narrative move that may suggest a radically different view of the functioning of desire than the tale of Promos and Cassandra. Although Philoxenus may be friendly to strangers, both by permitting the disputants of Whetstone's text to stay at his villa and permitting the Eastern characters of his Ionian tale to achieve a happy ending (these lovers are ultimately transformed into a pair of turtle doves [226]), the text as a whole is more reflective of the sexual violence that the tale of Promos and Cassandra suborns.

William Averell's *A Dyall for Dainty Darlings rockt in the cradle of Securitie: A Glasse for all disobedient Sonnes to looke in. A Myrrour for vertuous Maydes. A Booke right excellent, garnished with many woorthy examples, and learned aucthorities, most needefull for this tyme present* (1584) also uses the unleashing of violence against the female as a means of characterizing the abject Otherness of the East as a means of edifying its readers, both male and female. In a heavily moralized text (even more prone to moralizing digressions than Pettie's *Petite Palace*), his narrator tells us that

> in the example of a Captaines wife of Constantinople, whose detestable pride, was so lothsome in the eyes of the Lord, that it procured his iustice to worke reuenge vpon her stincking carcase. The report whereof as I haue breefely read, so the discourse thereof, I will shortly write, trusting that all these in whome the sparkes of vertue are kindled, will by her example growe into a greater increase of vertue, and they whome the water of follie hath quenched thyr good desyres, will warme themselues at the flames of wisedome, to drie vp the moisture of theyr vicious mindes. (9)

In other words, not only is the narrative true, but it will satisfy a didactic goal by teaching us the evils of pride, made more loathsome by being illustrated by a woman, the wife of a Venetian captain, living in the lymytrophall location of Constantinople. This woman is so proud that she refuses to bathe herself in common water or to feed herself. Eventually God punishes her, causing her body to rot in "euery parte of this her pampered body, so that no member, no joint, nor part therof was free from the mouldred plague of putrifaction" (12). The stench from her rotting body creates "an intollerable stincke" (13) that drives away all her friends and all but one of her servants. The bodily destruction and isolation she suffers here—which provides Averell with the opportunity to discuss the evils of pride and to exhort women "to auoide curiositie" (13)—is reminiscent of what Florinda/ Floride hoped she would achieve by the violence she inflicted upon herself, but in this case it is a Christian God who unleashes violence against the woman, who is placed in the Eastern context of Constantinople and whose own hedonistic desires are responsible for her suffering.

Tunisian Pirates and "Turning Turk"

More examples could be cited of early modern novellas in which the East similarly figures. It de-centers European, Christian values as they are present in the male, and it provides a "glasse" through which we may observe the effects of that de-centering as the unleashing of violent, unrestrained desire that threatens the female character—either at her own hand or that of a male figure tainted by the East. The female's action then becomes emblematic of the dangers of cultural annihilation that the East represents: Florinda and Carmosyna become violent against themselves, Carmosyna becomes economically active, the captain's wife endures an entirely pointless death. Within the didactic framework of collections of "histories" that, as Fenton puts it, are at least partly designed to encourage the "avodynge a present mischiefe, and preventynge any evil afore yt fall," the use of contact with the Turks provides a subtle attempt to educate early modern readers to the need to textually if not politically colonize the Ottoman Empire by reducing it to a threatening Other that would dehumanize all those who encountered it. Because of a variety of European cultural fears, provoked by the Reformation as well as by the Turks' military strength,[36] the Ottoman Empire became for writers and translators of novellas an essential imaginative location.

Another pair of collections, *The Cobbler of Canterbury* (1590), revised as *The Tinker of Turvey* (1630), also include a tale that occurs largely within the framework of the East, again showing the kind of cultural disruption that Eastern contact, even benevolent contact, can cause. This tale, the Scholar's tale about two young lovers who flee their warring families in Sicily and are captured by Tunisian pirates, begins thus:

When the King of Tunis was beaten out of his kingdom and sought to enter again by force, Jacomine Pierro and Alexander Bartolo, two noblemen of Sicilia, and both of Palermo, for the good will they bore the king, prepared certain tall barks, and with their aid, maugre his enemies, placed the king safe again in his kingdom. (175)[37]

After this initial reference to the East, the text focuses on the emerging love of the nobles' children, the family feud that erupts and keeps them apart, and the young lovers' decision to sail to Spain in order to be together. At sea they are captured by Tunisian pirates, the woman is transported to the seraglio of the King of Tunis, and her beloved roams dejectedly about the city looking for her until he spies her just before he is about to abandon hope and leave. He sneaks into her room and they consummate their marriage just before the King decides that it is time for him to come to her for the first time. The threat of the woman's rape by the Tunisian king is replaced by the threat of death for both lovers after the Tunisian king, who discovers the two Sicilians together in her bed, decrees that they shall be burned at the stake. This tortuous death is only forestalled by the recognition by the King's High Admiral that they are the offspring of the Italian defenders of the Tunisian monarch. At this point, the King pardons them and they thank him for his mercy. The young man is then knighted by the king, who provides them with a ship laden with treasure in which to sail home (182–83).

This Tunisian knighthood links the tale with that of Amadour and Florinda: like Painter's Amadour, the knight's return to the Christian West carries elements of the East with it. As in the other examples we have examined, in other words, contact with the Turk—here in the form of the earlier generous military support of the lovers' fathers—precedes the unleashing of unrestrained desire (we are given no explanation for the feud that erupts between the families). And this benevolent action has as its ultimate result the importation of a Tunisian noble (the knighted Italian) into Sicilian culture. Cultural annihilation is never discussed in the text, but the threat posed by this event echoes with a fear that Sir Philip Sidney expressed in a 1573 letter to Hubert Languet: *Nonne rides nos Saxones etiam jam Turkanifare?* or "Wouldn't you laugh if all Anglo-Saxons turned Turk?"[38]

3

"Full Works to Excellent Geographers"

THE SPACES OF ARCADIAN ROMANCE

It is the fear of "turning Turk" that drives a large proportion of ethnographic texts discussing Europe, North Africa, and Asia Minor.[1] The fear of Christendom's fall to the Ottoman Empire was considerable during the sixteenth century. Turkish incursions into Western Europe, as Bandello's dedication to his collection has already made clear, were a source of cultural anxiety, because of both the military strength of the Ottoman Turks and their association with the rejection of Christianity. The Battle of Lepanto in 1571 marked a turning point in Turkish military expansion, permitting Europe to breathe a little more easily, but Turkish power still generally remained a frightening source of Otherness, despite occasional references, such as in Barnaby Riche's in *Brusanus* (1592), to a time when the ruler Liberius ruled Constantinople and "parts of Cayre, Soria, Calypha, and all Grecia in the most christian and catholicke faith" (4). Greece and various other neighboring locations such as Cyprus are often represented in sixteenth-century ethnographic and travel texts as locations that Christianity has lost to Turkish control. This sense of the Ottoman Empire as poised to eradicate European cultural and religious identity, as well as to destroy the developing sense of national identities beginning to flourish in England and on the Continent, has particular ramifications for a text such as Sidney's *Arcadia,* which establishes itself less as a romance about lovers than as an analysis of a place itself, struggling to transform it into a lived space—to give it a "local habitation and a name"—even as it participates in the fantasy of de-materializing the province for which it is named; and which, moreover, asserts itself as a text for women. It thereby intimately links its analysis of Arcadian cultures with an analysis of women's imbrication in and response to the creation of cultural representation.[2]

In the second eclogues of the *Old Arcadia,* for instance, Pamela asks the aptly named Histor to describe

> what strange adventure it was that had led the two Greek princes from Erona, after they had slain Otanes and settled her in her kingdom. . . . Histor made answer that Plangus indeed had before his departure towards Thessalia and Macedon, at his importunate desire, made a brief declaration unto him thereof, but always with protestation that such things they were as many particularities of them had been full works to excellent historiographers. (*Old Arcadia* 134)

The heroic adventures Histor implies here contrast greatly with the report of one such historiographer, William Lithgow, whose *A Most Delectable, and Trve Discourse, of an admired and painefull peregrination from Scotland, to the most famous Kingdomes in Europe, Asia, and Affricke* (1614), describes his travels in Arcadia thus:

> Wee entred in the hilly and barren Countrey of *Arcadia;* where, for a dayes iourney we had no village, but saw aboundance of Cattell without keepers. In this Desart way, I beheld many singular monuments, and ruinous Castles, whose names I knew not, because I had an ignorant guide: But this I remember, amongst these rockes, my belly was pinched, and wearied was my body, with the climing of fastidious mountaines, which bred no small griefe to my breast. Yet notwithstanding of my distresse, the remembrance of these sweete seasoned Songs, of *Arcadian* Shepherds which pregnant Poets haue so well penned, did recreate my fatigated corps, with many sugred suppositions. These sterile bounds being past, wee entred in the Easterne plaine of *Morea.* (sig. E3ʳ⁻ᵛ)

As Lithgow's text explains, "Although in former times it was pleasant, yet it is now for the most part wast and disinhabited" (sig. E3ʳ⁻ᵛ). Lithgow must, it seems, describe Arcadia in simultaneously historical and fictive terms; he must be much more attuned to its figurative landscape than are historiographers describing other non-European locations. Although a much more symbiotic relationship exists between the fictional and nonfictional constructions of other locations—such as the European spaces the novellas create, for example, which in their attempts to create histories simultaneously create rich descriptions of fictional places or rely on a knowledge of nonfictional geography in order to establish the parameters of its fictional world[3]—Arcadian romances work to create a fictional place that then becomes transferred to the corresponding historical spaces. When Sidney and other writers who rely on Arcadia as a location for their texts appropriate the province, any tenuous link it had to geographical specificity seems to be lost—it is purely the desert Lithgow describes it as. As A. C. Hamilton, among others, has argued, the text draws on the depiction of Arcadia as represented in Sidney's major sources, particularly Sannazaro's *Arcadia*. The world of the beginning of Sidney's text highlights the difference between "the poet's ideal world and nature's real one, between what should be and what is. . . . It establishes Arcadia as removed from life, distant in time and place."[4] The distinction between the ideal and real worlds that Hamilton identifies parallels the distinction I am making, except that his terminology implies greater fictionality and a greater dichotomy than the text supports. In the Arcadian world, real and ideal, fictional and historical become conflated even as an attempt is made to distinguish the two. To write a romance set in Arcadia is to write a romance about Arcadia and to invoke its historical and fictive dimensions seamlessly.

Sidney's *Arcadia* in both its versions certainly provides the most important examples of this confluence, and scholarly attention has been previously drawn to the locations of Sidney's text. Jean Robertson, for instance, includes Mercator's relevant maps in her edition of the *Old Arcadia*.[5] Peter Lindenbaum published in 1984 a brief article called "The Geography of Sidney's *Arcadia*," which discusses Sidney's use of Mercator and Strabo and argues that the *New Arcadia* is much more geographically accurate than the original version of the text.[6] Alan Sinfield observes that the romance focuses on the "deeds of subaltern figures" without fully developing the implications of that statement.[7] More common, however, have been comments such as Elizabeth Dipple's, which erase much of the materiality of Arcadia in favor of seeing it as "a place where the heroic deeds possible in other lands are thwarted or radically changed in quality, intention, or effect."[8] However, an analysis of the specific implications of Arcadian geography, an analysis that explores the cultural associations that circulated in the early modern period about the places central to Sidney's text and others like it, will permit us to develop a more fully rounded picture of the polyvocal ways in which the Arcadian world would have resonated within early modern England and the ways in which these ethnographic and fictional glasses blend.

In fact, it seems virtually impossible to discuss the *Arcadia* without implying conclusions about its geography and cultural difference from Sidney's readers, regardless of how submerged those implications are. The retreat of Basilius and his family into the countryside at the romance's beginning makes its landscape significant if solely on a symbolic level; the romance's title, focusing on the site of action instead of the characters who act, transforms Arcadia into a kind of character itself. Further, as R. W. Maslen suggests, Pyrocles and Musidorus arrive in Arcadia "like Ascham's Italianate Englishmen or Lyly's Euphues . . . travelling to complete their education."[9] The revisions that Sidney made to his text further amplify and qualify our sense of Arcadia as a "space." Arguments such as Richard Berong's "Changing Attitudes toward Material Wealth in Sidney's *Arcadias*" trace the ways in which revisions to Sidney's romance are changes to the representation of Arcadian culture. Writing, for example, of the way in which the *Old Arcadia* depicts wealth, Berong states that "this is clearly a world where material wealth impresses." Arguments about the romance in critical discourse quickly become arguments about Arcadian culture itself.[10]

Sidney's famous opening of the *Old Arcadia* informs its readers that "Arcadia among all the provinces of Greece was ever had in singular reputation, partly for the sweetness of the air and other natural benefits, but principally for the moderate and well tempered minds of the people."(4). This opening, echoed by the initial emphasis on setting in such works as Gervase Markham's *The English Arcadia* (1607) and Emanuel Forde's *Parismus* (1598),[11] focuses initial attention on Arcadia as a geographical location—as one of "the provinces of Greece"—and initiates discussion of a series of locations throughout Greece, Asia Minor, and the Middle East: Cyprus, Macedon, Thessalia, Syria, and Persia, to name a few.

Although Sidney's text draws attention to Greece as a geographic location comprised of several provinces, it also emphasizes the qualities of Arcadia and its specific inhabitants. Strabo had emphasized that the tribes inhabiting Arcadia were among the most ancient of the Greeks, but references to Arcadia in contemporary geographic and ethnographic texts are few (certainly few are as extensive as Lithgow's), and they generally confirm Sidney's broad sketch of the place.[12] Thomas Floyd's *The Picture of a Perfit Common wealth . . . Gathered forth of many authors* (1600), for instance, includes a brief mention of Arcadia in a chapter titled "Of Peace," but only in discussion of its people, not as a geographic entity. The Arcadians in Floyd's discussion function by their absence, as the impetus for Archedamus, king of Lacedemonia, to reflect on the virtues of peace. Having beaten the Arcadians in battle, he observes,

> It had been better if wee had ouercome them by prudence, rather than by force: euery prince that desireth war, stirreth vp against himself, both the hatred and weapons of his neighbor, he vexeth his subiects vnworthily, seeking rather to rule ouer them by violence, then to gaine their good wil by iustice, he quite ouerthroweth his countrey.[13]

Arcadians here are both a cultural group and a symbolic force. They, through their military weakness, prompt an understanding of the virtues of peace and "prudence." The values of the Arcadian people prompt the Lacedemonian king to understand the symbolic value of peace—they do not stay fixed in the literal, geographic realm. The symbolic, idyllic nature of Arcadia is asserted more directly by a reference in Robert Allott's *Wits Theater of the Little World* (1599) to the scorpions of Arcadia as "gentle, and sparing of theyr naturall soyle."[14] Even the natural world of the province empathizes with the peaceful nature of the Arcadians (whom Allott, citing Strabo, calls "the best & first masters of defence" [sig.V8ᵛ–Xiʳ]). Nicolas de Nicholay's *The Navigations, Peregrinations and Voyages, made into Turkie* (1585) refers to Arcadia as the place where "Prometheus the sonne of Iapetus, who being a man of deep knowledge, taught the rude menne to liue ciuillie."[15] As these quotations suggest, references to Arcadia in sixteenth-century texts often preserve Arcadia's status as a distant, quasi-classical location. Moreover, it resonates as a location of unrealistic peace, calm, and civility. In its past incarnation it was a site of human achievement—where "rude menne" learned to establish civil government, but it was also a site of decay, where people may be conquered and where venomous animals exist, even if they do not harm their fellow Arcadians; it is both improbably idealized and corrupt. Interesting too in this context is Gynecia's association of her moral decline, that is, her lust for Philoclea, with geography: "O deserts, deserts, how fit a guest am I for you, since my heart is fuller of wild ravenous beasts than ever you were!" (80). Although Dipple would de-emphasize the role of literal geography in this passage, observing that the Arcadian retreat is "more reflective of her inner nature than was the former dignity

and artificial control of the court,"[16] Gynecia's outburst links her awareness of Arcadia to the kind of geographical specificity that Lithgow observed in his travels. Stripping her speech of its specific cultural context
prevents the full implications of the material content of Gynecia's language,
or of Arcadian spaces, from being recognized.[17]

Allusions to Greece more generally in Sidney's romance link it to the
classical past, but they also insist upon its contemporary status. Allott asserts Greece's political strength "so long as [the Greek provinces] continued at peace among themselues" (sig. K5^v); once dissension among Greeks
began, their political power waned, leading to sixteenth-century Greece's
subordination to Turkish control. George Abbot, in *A Briefe Description of
the Whole Worlde* (1599), for instance, emphasizes what Greece accomplished
"in olde time."[18] It is only in the last paragraph of his chapter about Greece
that he considers contemporary circumstances, stating, "By the great dis-
cord of Christians: all *Grecia,* and this Citie [Constantinople] is fallen into
the handes of the Turks. . . . The Christians that do liue now in *Grecia,* are
in miserable servitude vnto the Turke" (sig. Aviii^v). Robert Johnson's 1601
"epitome" translation of Giovanni Botero's *The Travellers Breviat,* to cite a
second example of this trend, states that all of Greece lies within the Turk's
"perambulation."[19] De Nicholay explains that Greeks "do abeisance vnto
the patriarch of Constantinople" (sig. Fi^v).

The significance of the Turkish link to Greece should not be underestimated. European anxiety over Turkish military prowess was common in the
sixteenth century, as was the association in the Christian West between Turks
and godlessness. Consequently, the "moderate and well-tempered" Arcadians
of Sidney's text exist simultaneously with Floyd's depiction of them as a people
separated from Christianity and whose oppression teaches their conqueror
to value peace. Their ancient glory, in other words, is marred by their sixteenth-century position. One effect of the simultaneous classical and contemporary perception of Arcadia and Greece is an increased suspicion of
Basilius's reign. His willingness to abandon the seat of his government casts
doubts upon his ability to rule, no matter in what context one reads his action; but seen in the context of contemporary discourse on the East, it seems
to be foreshadowing the downfall of Greece and its conquest by the Ottoman Empire. The other locations of Sidney's romance also become imbued
with this simultaneously fictive and ethnographic identity, creating our geographical understanding of them as they develop their romance implications.

Sidney's Other Arcadian Spaces: Gendered and Barbaric Geography

In Sidney's romance, Arcadia is not the only location multidimensionally developed. Cyprus also functions as a key site of both fictive and ethnographic importance, but it is not marked as a geographic destination, rather as a place associated with the female Gynecia and filled with magic and exotica. For instance, references to Cyprus link it with the bottle of love potion Gynecia administers to Basilius:

> She remembered the bottle, for it had been kept of a long time by the kings of Cyprus as a thing of rare virtue, and given to her by her mother when she being very young married to her husband of much greater age, her mother (persuaded it was a property to force love with love's effects) had made a precious present of it to this her well beloved child—though it had been received rather by tradition to have such a quality than by any approved experiment. (224)

We learn more about the potion itself after Basilius has begun to recover from its effects, and again Sidney ensures that we link the elixir with its origin in Cyprus. The "drink" had been developed because

> a princess of Cyprus, grandmother to Gynecia . . . did furiously love a young nobleman of her father's court, who fearing the king's rage, and not once daring either to attempt or accept so high a place, she made that sleeping drink, and found means by a trusty servant of hers . . . to procure him that suspected no such thing, to receive it. (415)

Because the potion proves efficacious in that instance, the princess "preserved in a bottle (made by singular art long to keep it without perishing) great quantity of it" (416). It may be worth noting here that this potion receives essentially two tales of origin: it is said to have power "by tradition" only, and not by experience, before it is administered; but after Basilius has received it, it is revealed to have had practical effect. It also seems to be linked to a later early modern example of a magic love token—Othello's handkerchief, which, while not created in Cyprus (if Othello's tale of the Egyptian charmer is to be believed—notice that that token also receives two tales of origin), does work its most powerful effects there. This association undoubtedly stems, at least in part, from Cyprus's classical association with Venus, as does its use in John Dickenson's *Arisbas* (1594), in which the lovers leave Venus's island when their love is thwarted and only return when their union may be sanctioned.

Cyprus figures in early modern accounts both in relation to its classical past and in the context of its subjection to the Turks.[20] As is well known, it had changed political hands often since the middle ages. Sir Anthony Sherley reported that when he and his company arrived at Cyprus, they

> found nothing to answere for famous relations giuen by ancient Histores of the excellency of that Iland, but the name onely, (the barbarousnesse of the Turke, and time, hauing defaced all the Monuments of Antiquity) no shew of splendor, no habitation of men in a fashion, nor possessors of the ground in a Principallity; but rather Slaues to cruell Maisters, or prisoners shut vp in diuers prisons: so grieuous is the burthen of that miserable people, and so deformed is the state of that Noble Realme.[21]

The "famous relations giuen by Ancient Histores" seems principally to refer to Cyprus's association in classical mythology with Venus. Richard Linche's 1599 translation of Vincenzo Cartari's *The Fountaine of Ancient Fiction,* a handbook describing classical deities and their properties, explains that to Venus

> was consecrated the Island of Ciprus, & especially in it the city of Paphos, for that she was seen and discouered vpon her first appearance out of the sea, to go on land on that part of the country: by reason whereof, the people therabouts adore and worship her with great zeale & veneration.[22]

Venus herself is described both as "the goddesse of wantonnes & amorous delight" who "inspired into the minds of men, libidinous desires, and lustfull appetites, & concupiscence" (sig. CCii[r]) and as a warrior who inspires women to maintain "manly courages, stoutnesse, and [resolution]" (sig. CCiv[r]).

A similarly complex system of associations is also present in an account published in Hakluyt's *Principal Navigations* (1598–1600), William Malim's translation of *The true report of all the successe of Famagusta, made by the Earle Nestor Martiningo, unto the renowned Prince of Venice,* which is accompanied by a dedicatory letter to the Earl of Leicester and a brief political history of Cyprus. Malim's prefatory material contains a certain degree of contempt: it refers to "those hellish Turkes,"[23] who are both the "horseleeches of Christian blood" (122) and the "ancient professed enemies to all Christian religion" (123), but the tone of the Italian report he translates is remarkably balanced, stressing the military strategies and prowess of both forces during the siege and eventual downfall of Famagusta.

Only at the close of the report does the tone shift to echo Malim's hatred. As Malim begins to describe the terms of surrender, terms that the Turks would not later respect, his marginal gloss to the text reads: "Just Turkish dealing, to speake and not to meane: sodainely to promise, and never to perform the same" (144). After the Venetian leader Bragadino has been captured and had his ears cut off, a second gloss defines the Turkish leader Mustafa as "cosin germaine to ye thiefe, which hong on the left side of our Saviour at his Passion" (146). Cyprus, in this account, becomes home to Greek peasants, Venetian overlords, and "those hellish Turkes" who seize it and encourage the peasants to leave its fields barren because they feel compelled to hide for fear of the "crueltie of the Turkes" (150). Abbot also emphasizes the subjection of Cyprus to the Turk (sig. D4^v), as does Botero (39). The 1568 translation of André Thevet's *The New found worlde* adds a different dimension to discussions of Cyprus and its people, citing Justinus for the report that the inhabitants of Cyprus, like the Lydians and the Armenians, had a custom of sending "theyr virgins and maidens to the sea borders, there in offering themselues to all commers to get them husbandes, or else their dowries [. . . and] when they were quit and well iustified, [they] offered to the Goddesse *Venus,* a present or offeryng."[24]

Aligning Gynecia with Cyprus, a geographic space simultaneously linked with Venus and the infidel Turk, complicates our understanding of her and her role in Sidney's romance. She is linked both to the island's associations with Venus and, as Thevet notes, with customs designed to stress sexual love and the means of attaining it, but her own origins as the King of Cyprus's daughter align her with those ruling Cyprus—the Turks. She comes from a family that rules over a "miserable people," to repeat Sherley's phrase, in a land "defaced" and dispossessed of its past glory—John Grange's *Golden Aphroditis* (1577), to cite another fictional text, refers to Cyprus when it was "yet unwasted"(53). If she is seen in this light, her marriage to Basilius furthers a sense of Arcadia's impending decay and more solidly links Arcadia's government with the Turkish opponents of Europe and Christianity. She becomes, then, part of the non-Western Other in need of colonialist control.

Other cultures in Sidney's *Arcadia* similarly become invested with the simultaneously fictive and ethnographic, although not the gendered, associations present in its representation of Cyprus. For instance, Macedon and Thessalia, the homes of Pyrocles and Musidorus, receive considerable treatment in the text. Macedon is characterized, at first obliquely, through the description of its king, Euarchus, as

> a prince of such justice that he never thought himself privileged by being a prince, nor did measure greatness by anything but goodness; as he did thereby root an awful love in his subjects towards him, so yet could he not avoid the assaults of envy—the enemy and yet the honour of virtue. (10)

We learn later that Euarchus "never forgot his office was to maintain the Macedonians in the exercise of goodness and happy enjoying their natural lives, never used war . . . but when it was to defend their right whereon their well being depended" (358). Thessalia functions as the location to which Musidorus sends the shepherd with whom he changes clothing early in the romance, providing with him sealed orders that he should be arrested and imprisoned until Musidorus countermands the order (41). We also learn, after the eloping Musidorus and Pamela have been apprehended, that Thessalia is a location that Musidorus expected "should have yielded" itself to Pamela (311)—in other words, it is a place that would have welcomed a princess breaking her own country's laws. During the trial that concludes the *Old Arcadia*, Thessalia also receives Musidorus's criticism for its role in Pyrocles's downfall in Arcadia:

> How unhappy may I think Thessalia that hath been as it were the middle way to this evil state of yours. For if you had not been there brought up, the sea should not have had this power thus to sever you from your dear father. I have therefore (if complaints do at any time become a man's heart) most cause to complain, since my country, which received the honour of Pyrocles' education, should be a step to his overthrow—if human chances can be counted an overthrow to him that stands upon virtue. (370–71)

Pyrocles later defends Thessalia in a similar vein, arguing during the trial before Euarchus that there would be terrible consequences should Musidorus be sentenced to death:

O give not such an occasion to the noble Thessalians for ever to curse the match that their prince did make with the Macedonian blood. By my loss there follows no public loss, for you are to hold the seat, and to provide yourself perchance of a worthier successor. But how can you, or all the earth, recompense the damage that poor Thessalia shall sustain, who sending out (whom otherwise they would no more have spared than their own eyes) their prince to you, and you requesting to have him, by you he should thus dishonourably be extinguished? (414)

Both Thessalia and Macedon, in other words, are usually yoked together and are usually invoked as seats of nobility and civilization. Although Macedon receives a bit more specific attention, because of Euarchus's role as the judge of Book 5's trial, both locations are at least superficially aligned with the noble princes and with justice (although Thessalia is the location of the shepherd Menalcas's wrongful imprisonment). Both are places rightly proud of their princes.[25]

Contemporary sixteenth-century references to Thessalia and Macedon mention, but not in an unqualified manner, their emphasis on nobility and justice, linking them to the characterizations of Arcadia already discussed.[26] De Nicholay states that in "times past [the Macedonians] were amongst the other Graecians in feats of warre most valiant and flourishing" (sig. V8r). However, "vainglory and arrogancy" took the place of the "most honest government, which they had in their common wealth," and their country fell into "a life disordered, corrupted, and full of al villainy, and abhominable dissolution" (sig. V8v). Allott describes the conquering of Macedonia by Mohammed (sig. Aa8r) and Alexander's marrying off the nobles of Macedonia to "the Ladies of Persia" (sig. G7r) and further cites King Philip of Macedon's vowing "his sonne vnto Aristotle as soone as euer he was born" as an example of an individual recognizing the value of education (sig. H7v). Botero emphasizes that the province is currently controlled by the Turks. The use of these two places in Sidney's text as locations that will receive fugitives from Arcadia, or that will imprison the shepherd Menalcas without substantial motivation, casts suspicion on these two sites. These

suspicions are augmented by sixteenth-century links between these locations, "abhominable dissolution," and colonization by the Turks: they become simultaneously idealized in their fictionalized past and colonized in
their historicized present. At the same time, Sidney's readers are invited to
focus on that idealized, fictionalized past marked by the justice of Euarchus
and to diminish the Turkish associations of current history. They are asked
to consider the idealized past as the historical present so as to diminish the
threat to European culture that the colonization of these texts creates.

Other locations Sidney discusses in the *Old Arcadia* function in a similar
way. Thrace, for instance, appears in the romance as a country whose forces
invade Macedon and over which Pyrocles is ultimately given control. In the
period's ethnographic texts, it is aligned with the Turks. Botero acknowledges
that it is under Turkish control, but, he says, "What prouince is richer in corne
then Egypt, Africke, Syria and Asia? What region more flowing with all good
things then Hungarie, Greece, and Thrace?" (39). Epirus, another country
whose troups invade Macedon in Sidney's romance, is called in Thomas
Procter's *Of the Knowledge and Conducte of Warres* (1578) a "little Countrey Epirus
in Grecia [that] resisted the huge and grosse powers of the greate Turke."[27]
Syria, Lycia, and Paphlagonia are similarly called, in Allott's *Wits Theater* (sig.
Aa7r) and in William Watreman's translation of Johannes Boemus's *Omnium
Gentium Mores* (1555), locations under Turkish control.[28] Linking Pyrocles to
Turkish-controlled locations emphasizes his separation from the European
West even as it promotes the fantasy of a Europeanized, Christianized East.

The distance between Sidney's European readers and the East is further
emphasized by the portion of the *Old Arcadia* that contains a concentration
of geographical references: the tale of Erona, which is told to the shepherd
Histor by the "Iberian nobleman" (67), Plangus. Erona, princess of Lydia,[29]
refuses to marry Otanes, king of Persia, because of her love for a lowly
court servant, Antiphilus. Her rejection of Otanes prompts her father to
die brokenhearted and, after his death, spurs Otanes to wage war against
Lydia. When Erona has been captured by Otanes "in her best city" (68),
Pyrocles and Musidorus, driven by a tempest, arrive in Lydia. During what
we learn is their first adventure, they fight to free Erona "as well to help the
weaker as for the natural hate the Grecians bare the Persians" (68). After
Otanes is killed, his sister, Artaxia, becomes queen of Persia, and Plangus
conducts her "in safety to her country" (69). After the war, Antiphilus marries Erona "against the consent of all the Lydian nobility" (69), but he has
fallen in love with Artaxia. Consequently, he plots with Artaxia to kill Erona

and allow Persia to subdue Lydia. Artaxia double-crosses Antiphilus, imprisons Erona, and has Antiphilus put to death.

At this point in the narrative during the first eclogues, it is revealed that Artaxia has vowed that Erona will be put to death if Pyrocles and Musidorus do not return to Persia within four years to battle her four champions and, as she surmises, to be killed by them in revenge for their killing of her brother. Artaxia sends Plangus to search for the two princes who, as we are told, "in this mean time, had done such famous acts that all Asia was full of their histories" (70). He searches through Egypt and Greece (and particularly in "the south part of the Peloponnesus" [71]), where the shepherd Histor overheard Plangus's tale), and he plans to continue his search into Thessalia and Macedon. If those countries do not harbor them, he will return to Persia.

During the second eclogues, the story of Erona is resumed—first because of Cleophila's request to hear the Plangus's poetic lament, a poem that, incidentally, is void of geographical allusion; second, because Pamela desires to hear the further adventures of Pyrocles and Musidorus. Their exploits, according to Plangus, would constitute "full works to excellent historiographers" (153). These adventures take them into Paphlagonia, where they help a people tyrannized by a giant and a dragon in a castle; into Syria and Damascus, where they settle rival brothers' claims to the throne, "making the brothers see the shamefulness" (154) of their contention with each other; and into Arabia at the request of "the great lady of Palestina" who has been abandoned by "a young prince of Arabia" (154). The princes flee Arabia for Egypt after having been imprisoned by the Palestinian lady, whose love they both reject.

They select Egypt as a destination in large part because "they heard great fame of the king of Egypt's court, to be by reason of his magnificence full of valiant knights, as also his country well policied with good laws and customs, worthy to be learned" (155). There they become involved with saving a Hippolytus figure and his look-alike servant from the lustful machinations of a Phaedra-like stepmother. Having restored the two young men to their rightful positions, Pyrocles and Musidorus "returned, as it was thought, Greece-ward" (158). Plangus's final hope in finding the princes, he asserts, is to locate them in one of their home countries. We hear of these events and their locations again only in the final paragraph of the text, when the narrator informs us:

But the solemnities of these marriages, with the Arcadian pastorals full of many comical adventures happening to those rural lovers, the strange story of the fair queens Artaxia of Persia and Erona of Lydia, with the prince Plangus's wonderful chances, whom the latter had sent to Pyrocles, and the extreme affection Amasis, king of Egypt, bare unto the former, . . . may awake some other spirit to exercise his pen in that wherewith mine is already dulled. (417)

In geographic terms, two points merit notice about this conclusion. First, never in the *Old Arcadia* is the tale of Erona resolved; she still faces either death or rescue by Pyrocles and Musidorus. In addition, the geography that had dominated the embedded tale of the princes' early adventures receives considerable emphasis as the text draws to a close. Our attention is drawn as much to Egypt as it is to the loves of the shepherds of the eclogues and to the "admirable fortunes" of the children of the two princely couples.

Abbot's *A Brief Description of the Whole Worlde* identifies Lydia as the place "where reigned sometimes Craesus, who was so renowned for his aboundant riches" (sig. Bvi^v), and other references to it seem to be equally anecdotal (references, in other words, are not made to the nature of its present rulers). Thevet describes the Lydian custom of sending maidens to the shore to find husbands, a custom that is also ascribed, as we have seen, to Cyprian maidens; Allott, citing Plutarch, asserts that in past time the Lydians sentenced murderers to be galley slaves, but that they "confined those that were detracters and ill tongued men into a secret place, farre of from all company, the space of halfe a yeare" (sig. R7^v).

Persia, as might be expected, receives much more detailed—and more varied—discussion. Strabo had identified Persia as a country that had conquered Lydia (7.187) and, further, he had asserted that the Persians became "most famous amongst the Greeks, because none of the other barbarians who ruled Asia ruled Greeks" (7.187). In the sixteenth century, Boemus asserts that Persians

thought it fondenes in the Grekes, worthie to be laughed at, to imagine goddes to be sprong vp of menne. What so euer was dishonest to be done, that thoughte thei not honest to be spoke[n]. To be in debt was muche dishonour, but of all thinges most vile for to lie. (sig. Kvii^v)

He also asserts that in times past "the children there, by an ordenaunce no where elles vsed: doe carnally knowe their mothers" (sig. Kvii^r). Allott does not mention that second custom, but he does inform his readers that

Persians deprive liars of "all honour and farther speech" (sig. Q9ᵛ); that they value education (sig. H6ʳ); that, according to Pausanias, Persian priests eat no flesh and drink no wine (sig. E7ᵛ); that Persians kings handled the most important matters personally, leaving their princes to handle more mundane affairs (sig. Y3ᵛ); and that the Turks had at one time controlled the Persians (sig. Aa7ᵛ). Abbot reminds us that

> the people of this nation, although they were in former times very riotous, by reason of their great wealth: yet after they lost their Monerchie by the *Macedonians,* they haue growne great souldiers: and therfore, as they euer did strongly defend themselues against the olde Romaines. . . . And of late times, they haue strongly opposed themselues against the Turkes, euer making partie good with them. . . . The Persians are all this day Saracens in religion, beleeueing on Mahomet: but as Papistes and Protestants doe differ in opinion, concerning the same Christ: so doe the Turkes, and Persians about their *Mahomet:* the one pursuing the other as heretickes with most deadly hatred. Insomu[c]h, that there be in this respect, almost continuall warres betweene the Turkes and the Persians. (sig. Bivᵛ)

Thomas Newton's translation of Coelio Augustinus Curio's *A Notable Historie of the Saracens* (1575) observes that "the *Saracenes* expulsing the *Turks,* began agayne to raigne in *Persia,* in the yeere after the nauitie of our Sauiour Christe 1500. and there do raigne tyll this day" (sig. Kkiʳ).[30] Botero emphasizes the differences between the Persians and the Turks, claiming that the Turks have greater military discipline than the Persians (49), but that the Persians are extremely noble people "and in all kinde of ciuiltie and curtesie excell" Turkish culture (150). Procter adopts a broadly similar strain in his references to the Persians, saying that they are devoted to the "delicate life" (pref.) and are "sonke in delicate pleasures and in intemperance" (sig. Bivʳ). De Nicholay echoes these sentiments in the chapter "Of the wanton and voluptuous life of the Persians," in which the Persians "now adayes contrary to their auncient customes, are much giuen to all pleasure and voluptuousnesse, apparrelling themselues very sumptuously" (sig. Qiʳ).[31] He also informs us that Persian men are permitted to have several wives and that, despite their hedonistic ways, his personal impression of them is that they are "more noble, more ciuil, more liberall, and of better spirite and iudgement then the Turkes" (sig. Qiʳ). This view is contradicted by Anthony

Jenkinson, who in an account collected in Haklyut's *Voyages* calls them "soone angrie, craftie and hard people" (3.36).³²

Allott identifies Arabia as the birthplace of Mohammed (sig. A6ʳ), as do Abbot (sig. C2ʳ) and Curio (sig. D1ʳ). Botero writes that the Arabs under Turkish control hate the Turk for religious reasons (sig. H3ʳ), and he asserts that the Arabians have "obscured" Persia's reputation in the following way: "to bury in obliuion the memorie of their [the Persians'] former reputation, enacted by law that they should no more be called Persians but Saracens" (sig. Viᵛ). Thevet characterizes the complexion of Arabians, like that of Egyptians, as being "betwene blacke and white" (sig. Cviᵛ), as does de Nicholay (sig. Q6ʳᵛ), who also asserts that the inhabitants of Arabia Felix are very martial (sig. Q6ᵛ). The same vagueness about complexion is repeated by Leo Africanus—but of Egyptians. Leo calls the "countrey people" of Egypt "swart and browne" in color, but says that "the citizens are white."³³ Thevet further asserts that Arabians are as cruel as Turks (sig. Iiʳ), take many wives (sig. Kiᵛ), and never build but "stray around here and there like vagabundes" (sig. Kiʳ⁻ᵛ).

Egyptians are referred to in *The Fardle of Facions* as the people who "firste of all other, deuised the names of the twelue Goddes" (sig. Cviiᵛ). Their kings, he also reports, strictly follow their own laws (sig. Diiʳ) and demonstrate such "vprightnes towarde their sub[jec]tes" that Egyptians care more about "the health and the welfare of the Kyng, then for their wiues" (sig. Divʳ). Boemus also mentions, among other things, that Egyptians permit males to have more than one wife (sig. Eiiᵛ)—a point also made by Thevet (sig. Kiiʳ). Allott also emphasizes the Egyptian concern for justice, although he cites Pausanias to make clear that he is speaking of the ancient Egyptians (sig. D3ᵛ). He cites a few of their laws in other contexts: that liars are punished by death (sig. Q8ᵛ); that male adulterers are castrated, whereas female adulterers lose their noses (sig. Ll8ʳ); that their priests, "seruing false gods," may eat no meat and drink no wine (sig. E7ᵛ). He also reports that the Mahometan ruler, Ahumar, conquered Egypt (sig. A7ʳ) and that the Turkish sultan, Zelimus, "slew the Sultan of Egypt" (sig. A8ᵛ). Botero and Abbot also emphasize Egypt's subjection to Turkish control (sig. F4ʳ and sig. Civᵛ, respectively). Abbot additionally reports that Egyptians have always valued learning, especially in the fields of astronomy and mathematics (sig. Civʳ). Procter, on the other hand, says they "are founde more geuen to superstitions and idolatrie, then other nations" (pref., iiiʳ). And Leo Africanus adds that the inhabitants of Cairo are "merrie, iocund, and cheerful, [and they] will promise much but performe little" (313).

Again, the vaguely classical locations of the Erona tale become enmeshed in the colonizing discourse that surrounds Egypt, Arabia, Syria, and Persia in sixteenth-century ethnographic texts. As his readers meet the adventures of the heroic princes—adventures told in large part to inform Philoclea and Pamela of the grand deeds of their beloveds—they simultaneously read the locations that surround the characters and events as alien sites, sites populated by dissolute peoples, infidel pagans, and barbarous Turks. As such, their experience of the text is twofold: reading the narrative of the text, they erase the geographic reality of the locations that Sidney describes through an acceptance of the classical nature of the Arcadian tradition in which he writes; reading the text in geographic terms, they participate in the colonialist discourse that the text encourages. Their only textually authorized choices are to accept the fictional, classical view or to accept the distortions promoted by Christian writers such as Botero, de Nicholay, and Abbot. As has been argued, although the heroic princes of the text become increasingly powerless and unable to learn during the course of the romance, readers learn through the "negative *exemplum*" the princes provide.[34] The "moderate and well-tempered minds" of Sidney's readers become complicit with the text's colonizing impulses, impulses emphasized by the text's conclusion. The tales of Artaxia, Queen of Persia; Erona, Queen of Lydia; and Amasis, King of Egypt are not concluded, and our attention is drawn to the geographical spreading out of the *Old Arcadia*'s major characters. With that diaspora comes the colonizing assurance that such figures as Pyrocles, Musidorus, and their children will be able to repel the Turkish threat imperiling Christianity.

Arisbas, *the Arcadian Landscape, and the Nature of Poetry*

Other fictional texts cast the locations of Arcadian romance in intriguing ways that build upon the nonfictional representations the ethnographic texts claim to provide. Robert Greene's *Menaphon: Camillas alarum to slumbering Euphues* (1589), for example, is also set in Arcadia.[35] Here too it is a place inhabited by shepherds and subject to the actions of a wrathful Jove who has sent it a "noysome pestilence" (19), a suspect king (one who casts his daughter adrift only to later abduct and attempt—albeit unwittingly—to seduce her), and the oracular pronouncements of Apollo. It is also, in short, sinister—a place of spectacularly mistaken identities (the heroine doesn't realize she is being wooed by her presumed-dead husband or by her son [though she does recognize her father]), but what interests me about the text in the context of the current discussion is the way in which discourse surrounding the events of the romance is couched in terms of the language of historiographers. The running header throughout the text is "The reports of the Shepheards,"[36] which may, as David Margolies suggests, indicate Greene's appeals to "realism," but it also links the text with a specific, geographic kind of authority, with an attempt to cross genre boundaries in order to establish his romance as nonfictional, which, although related, is different from attempting to create realistic fiction. Such a sense of boundary crossing is further emphasized by two specific moments in the text. In the first, the narrator leaves unexplained some details of the childhood behavior of the heroine's son, deciding instead to "referre it to the Annuals of the Arcadians" (57). Later, the narrator skips over some of the arguments that the now adolescent son uses when he is trying to woo his mother, explaining that these are things "which the Arcadian Records doo not shew" (73). Such comments construct Arcadia as a location with a historical dimension, a dimension that is controlled by the fictional characters themselves; it is, after all, the shepherds who construct the reports on which the romance is based. Greene does not provide great detail about the cultural practices of the Arcadian shepherds, although we do witness their meetings and overhear an eclogue competition. We are, however, provided with a few cultural details, learning, for example, that Arcadia is "famous for the beautie of our Nymphes, & the amorous roundelaies of our shepheaeds [*sic*]" (46) and that it became the subject of the proverbial phrase *"No heaven but Arcadie"* (71). The other location that the text inhabits, Thessaly, remains equally undescribed, as does Cyprus, which functions only fictionally as the location that the disguised heroine, echoing Sidney's Gynecia, claims to be from.

Another romance that uses the Arcadian landscape in such a way as to blur distinctions between fiction and historiography is John Dickenson's *Arisbas, Euphues amidst his Slumbers* (1594), which owes more to Sidney than to Lyly despite its subtitle.[37] It tells the story of a Prince of Cyprus, Arisbas, and his bride Timoclea, who seek refuge from his unhappy father in Arcadia. The couple's rather straightforward plan is complicated by the ocean tempest that strands him on land while carrying her away, so that he is forced to search for her throughout the islands of the Ionian and Aegean Seas, Epirus, the Hellespont, Macedon, Thessaly, Thrace, and finally Arcadia, where he hears of a beautiful young man who has recently come to Arcadia, sparking desire in men and women alike. This young man is, of course, eventually revealed to be Timoclea herself, who tells of her adventures that involve shipwreck and abduction by two different sets of pirates and travels through the Hellespont, Byzantium, Laconia, Lacedemonia, and Syria before her escape into Arcadia. The lovers are reunited and return to Cyprus, where they learn that his father no longer objects to their marriage.

The text's links to Sidney have been noted by Salzman, who cites the Sidneian echoes in the name of Timoclea and a poem that Arisbas composes, which includes a reference to Pyrocles's disguising himself as Zelmane for the love of Philoclea (48), and the text's emphasis on the pastoral world even while it avoids the kind of philosophical debate and dialogue that mark Sidney's or Lyly's texts.[38] What is most relevant to our discussion of Dickenson's romance, however, is the dynamics of the relationship between Arcadia and Cyprus as geographical entities. Generally, the geographic movement on the diagetic level, that is, the dramatized events that occur in the romance's current time, of Sidney's *Arcadia,* especially of the *Old Arcadia,* is small. The action of the primary narrative is largely restricted to Arcadia—and even more to the pastoral portions of that province. Except for Kalender's house, the woodland lodges in which members of Basilius's family reside, and the town to which Miso is sent by Musidorus, the *Old Arcadia* is set in a bucolic landscape that goes largely undescribed beyond its initial characterization that focuses on the nature of its inhabitants rather than its topographic specificity. Of course, the tales of the princes' travels, of Argalus and Parthenia, and of Plangus and Erona, broaden the scope of the romance's geography, as do additional references to other locations, but the Arcadia of *Arcadia* remains a constricted, amorphous place. It is a location, as has been widely recognized, of political isolationism (since it becomes enmeshed in Basilius's flight from his civic responsibilities) described not in any geographic or ethnographic terms. We only get small glimpses of the countryside in such scenes as the moment when Pyrocles and Musidorus save Basilius's family from the attacks of the lion and the bear, when Pyrocles observes the bathing princesses, or when Mopsa and Dametas focus on the oak tree about which Musidorus has created his diversionary fictions.

The geographic movement of *Arisbas* suggests a different function of Arcadia. In this text the geographic movement is circular: from Cyprus to Arcadia and back to Cyprus.[39] Arcadia again functions as a refuge from

political engagement, though in this case the retreating couple is not a ruling pair. Arisbas is the son of a sitting king, and Timoclea is not a princess
but the daughter of an exiled noble from Epirus. And again it receives little
physical description; it instead becomes a site for the description of poetry,
pastoral reflection, and sexual confusion. More importantly, its descriptive
elements are drawn from Sidney's *Arcadia* and not from nonfictional texts.
Three elements of Sidneian influence stand out in this context: the allusion
to Pyrocles previously discussed, the naming of the festival at which
Timoclea's identity is revealed after Sidney's Parthenia, and the general
emphasis on cross-dressing throughout the text.

In a poem titled "Cupid's Palace," written while he awaits the day of the
feast at which the disguised Timoclea is to appear, Arisbas includes the following lines:

> Pyrocles such fancie knew,
> Fancie giuing Loue his due,
> Which did on Philoclea looke,
> Bathing in a Christall brooke.
> He disguisde a virgin seemd,
> And his name was Zelmane deemd.
> O how sweetly did he praise,
> In those lines those louely laies,
> All perfections in her planted?
> For his pen no praises wanted.
> Tresses of her Ambre haire,
> Wauing in the wanton aire.
> Rubie lips and corall chin,
> Soft, smooth, Alablaster skin.
> Angels iookes, hands lily white,
> Eyes subduing at the sight. (48–49)

What is important here is that Dickenson has Arisbas import not only the
names of Sidney's characters but also references to the bathing scene of the
Old Arcadia itself, which provide us with material for a description not only
of Philoclea herself but also with some physical description of the Arcadian
landscape. Admittedly, the scene does not provide a great deal of physical
description of place—we only learn that there is a "Christall brooke"—but it

is enough to evoke a visual image of the scene, even as it is enough to prompt a blazon describing Philoclea's beauties.

The second Sidneian borrowing in which Dickenson engages is his naming of the Feast of Parthenia. The text describes a dispute between the gods Zephyrus and Pomona for the love of a beautiful young man, Hyalus. Zephyrus enlists the aid of Boreas in obtaining Hyalus, who has been captured and imprisoned by Pomona in her castle in Arcadia:

> In this impatient humour, he [Zephyrus] hasted to the Northern regions, and meeting there with Boreas, saluted him thus. Father of stormes, salue now the sorrowes of vnhappy Zephyrus, thy brother in nature, thy equall in substance: helpe me, and for euer haue me a friend, a fauourer. I haue in one iniurie receiued more wrongs then I can reckon. Unmindfull, vnthankfull Arcadia not weighing the many fauours by mee affoorded, withholds from me my loue, my life, my hope, my heauen: but if thou powre thy plagues on that vnkinde soyle, and oppresse the inhabitants with outragious furie of thy blasts, my riuall may repent her rashnesse, and I recouer my losse. (40)

Pomona's actions become ascribed to Arcadia as a whole in this passage. It becomes "Unmindfull, vnthankfull"—an echo and an inversion of Sidney's characterization of his Arcadians, who possess "moderate and well-tempered minds" (*Old Arcadia* 4)—and is itself implicated in the actions of the possessive and lusty goddess. Boreas responds in kind:

> Boreas forthwith issute from his icy prouince with a troupe of tempests and inuaded Arcadia, where he wrought so many mischieues in a moment, that no eye could viewe them tearelesse. Groues were disgarnished of their shrubs, fields disfurnished of their floures: trees, some torne, some rent vp by the rootes, cattaile violently carried from the places where they fed, and tumbled headlong downe the cliffes, men staggering, could not stay their steps, leauing therefore their wonted walkes they housed themselues. (41)

The displeasure of Zephyrus becomes translated into language that describes the physical Arcadian countryside. It becomes a space we know visually, but only through the mythological agency of Boreas. Boreas's actions against the province do have their desired effect. Hyalus becomes freed from Pomona's control, and at this point the narrative becomes miraculous and even more overtly Sidneian:

> Hyalus set free, raunged in a childish rage, but being weary with wandering, he rested neere a pleasant Spring, and hauing wept freely, slept soundly. In this sleepe, strange sleepe, the late sexe was changed, and of a faire boy a fairer maide fashioned. Awaking and musing much at this metamorphosis, she was in the midst of her dumps raisde with a strong gale, & carried to a place neere the streights of Thermopyles, where was a Temple dedicated to Æolus, wherein the louely maide was consecrated a Priest to that God, and continued there the whole tearme of her life a spotlesse virgin. Our auncestors desirous to celebrate the remembrance of this rare accident with eternall honor, appointed the day of her change to be for euer, memorizd in a yearely feast called Parthenia, wherein the Priest of Æolus accompanyed with the fairest of the youth of both sexes, offers a noble Sacrifice, disposing all things with due Ceremonies. Which done, they compassing the aultar in a ring, sing a solemne Hymne in prayse of that God. This did our auncestors institute, and their progeny hath by long successe of time obserued their deuoute orders. (42)

Hyalus's sexual transformation provides Dickenson with a moment that is both Sidneian and ethnographic. The feast is named Parthenia, presumably because of connections between the root meaning of the word, "maiden," and the transformation Hyalus has undergone, but with the inescapable reference to Sidney's Parthenia who, after the death of her beloved Argalus, transforms herself into the male Knight of the Tomb in Book 3 of the revised *Arcadia*. The feast itself is described in the kind of detail we have seen nonfictional texts accord to the description of non-English cultures and customs, transforming Dickenson's romance momentarily from a fictional narrative into a kind of didactic traveler's report.

The broadest point of influence of Sidney's text on Dickenson's is apparent in the cross-dressing of Timoclea. Timoclea's masquerade as a male is alluded to more than seen: nearly from the moment that we learn of the presence in the south of Arcadia of the beautiful young man who wins the admiration of "lusty Gallants and dainty Girles" (27) and who prompts one Arcadian to "dot[e] more deeply then became a Neateheard" (27), Arisbas

suspects that this is Timoclea in disguise. We learn of the neatheard Dorylus's passion for him as we wait for him to appear at the feast of Parthenia.
Once he arrives on the scene, the disguise is quickly revealed, and Dickenson
prevents us from actually having to confront the cross-dressed figure directly. While we learn of Dorylus's love for the young man and read the
poems he writes to him, much as we read Pyrocles's poetry about Philoclea,
we do not confront the cross-dressed Timoclea for an extended period in
the narrative, nor are we led to ascribe any homosexual desire to Timoclea.
Although Dorylus's desires are termed excessive, the object of those desires rejects Dorylus so resoundingly that his fate becomes proverbial in
Arcadia. The narrator reports that "we term il successe in loue the destinie
of Dorylus" (33), a phrasing that again links Dickenson's narrative to the
rhetoric of the ethnographic report. Again, what happens in this moment
is that Dickenson's text crosses over from romance to ethnography, expli-
cating for us the origins of an alleged cultural idiom even as it flaunts its
Sidneian conventions.

One final moment in Dickenson's text also reveals the ways in which the
generic boundaries become crossed within this text. As has already been
noted, while Arisbas waits for the festival of Parthenia, he composes poetry
that is presented to the reader. The last of these poems,[40] "The worth of
Poesie" (49–52), prompts a discussion of poetry and its fate in the post-
Classical world, explaining where "Poesy" may currently be found:

> Poesy warning thence her golden wings beyond the Alpes, though
> returning, establisht an habit of high humors in France, the happy
> nourse of many rare spirits, which likewise with no lesse praise haue
> in liuely colours expressed all perfections of Poetry, and these being
> in like sort famous, neede not to be by me memorized. To these adde
> the labors of Castilian pens. But in Albion the wonder of Ilands louely
> Thamesis, fairest of the faire Nereides loues sea-borne Queene ador-
> ing, vaunts the glory of her maiden streames, happy harbour of so
> many Swans, Apollos musical birds, which warble wonders of worth,
> and chaunt pleasures choise in seuerall sounds of sweetnesse, pleas-
> ant, passionate, loftie, louely, whose matchlesse notes, the faire Nymph
> keeping tyme with the billowing of her Chrystall waues, carrying to
> the Ocean with her ebbe, doth there echo them to her astonisht sisters
> which assemble in those vast flouds by timely confluence. Bætis grac'd
> with many bounties, Po, and Arno, garnishd with many pleasures,

Rhone, and Araris, enriched with many royalties, yet none of these
may vaunt more heauens of happinesse then Thamesis, in harbouring
such Swans, such sweetnesse. Yet many most worthy monuments of
heauenly wits wanted the honor and safetie of this seate, for they
were drowned in the abysse of Lethes silence, especially of the most
ancient Græcian Authors, as Orpheus, Linus, the first Musæus, Aratus,
Nicander, Theognis, Phocilides, and most of all the nine Lyriques,
and Elegiacke and Comicke Poets, and some taskes of tragique pens,
with the precious predictions of the tenne Sybills, and many of the
Romane Worthies. Little remaines of graue Ennius, who vaunted
though vainegloriously the transmigration of great Homers soule,
seeking aduantage by that one poynt of Pythagorean doctrine to bol-
ster his owne ambition, but though he were rude in stile (which was
the fault of his time) yet was he graue in matter, and in this meriting
praise, that being one of those that brake the first yee, he rowsde the
following rare spirits. But worse hap befell the rare Smyrna of learned
Cinna, and sugred passions of sweete Gallus, and of those other both
Greeke and Romane workes, many are blemishde with some blurs:
so that it was high time that Phoebus and the Muses should vndertake
their protection, and become their patrones. But leauing this digression, let vs returne to the matter. (53–55)

Digression though it may be, it reveals again the ways in which the generic boundaries of the text become blurred and the ways in which geography and nonfictional discourse on location become embedded within the
fictional romance. The textual time filler of poetry composed ostensibly to
let the characters (and the readers) pass narrative time becomes the occasion not only for a discussion of the nature of poetry, such as we might
expect to find in Puttenham's *The Art of English Poesy* or Gascoine's *Certayne
Notes of Instruction,* but also of the geographic and nationalistic implications of such a discussion. The description of place becomes embedded
within the romance text, making it, albeit temporarily, a locus for the creation of norms about nonfictional cultures and cultural concerns: learning
about poetry means learning not only *what* it is but also *where* it is.

4

Trapalonia, Machilenta, and the Uses of Fictional "Glasses"

Knowledge of place is central to knowledge of content: that is what *Arisbas*'s discussion of poetry asserts (and sections of Sidney's *Apology for Poetry,* Nashe's "Preface" to *Menaphon,* and many other examples of early modern critical discourse could be cited as participating in the same aesthetic and epistemological impulse). There is an overwhelming desire to "locate" knowledge, to map it in spatial and geographic terms. This drive is apparent in an example common to any academic professional's experience: during those horrendous national job searches conducted while working on our dissertations, most of us applied for positions at colleges and universities we and our friends had never heard of—and even if we had, odds were good that our nonacademic family and friends had not. When we mentioned to them our recently sent off application to "Unknown U.," the most frequent response that we would receive was "Where's that?" We were not asked, "What's its Carnegie classification?" or "How many English majors does it have?" or any other question that might actually provide insight into the nature of the job that we would be asked to perform at the institution. It is a question analogous to the first question our culture asks about any newborn baby: "Is it a boy or a girl?" Gender and geography become the two central "glasses" through which the world becomes known, and these two categories become conflated in the tales of romance heroines whose kingdom of origin and gender are disguised. Dickenson's obscuring of Timoclea's gender and ethnicity then makes her emblematic of pervasive epistemological issues that drive early modern fiction and its ethnographic impulse. Knowing where women come from is central to controlling geographic space. And defining and controlling space is essential to the intertwined projects of Arcadian romance, colonialism, and ethnography. The impulse toward ethnography becomes so integrated into Sidney's romance that geographic space becomes, in a sense, the central character of the romance, and the obscuring of gender and geographic origins is of primary importance for the male characters as well as the female characters.

The subsumption of geographic concerns into the concerns of early modern romance becomes developed in additional ways during the period as well. In the texts that will be considered in the following discussion, the significance of geographical spaces becomes highlighted through its inversion: through the creation of geographic fictions that are perceived as such by the texts' readers, if not the fictional characters themselves. Robert Greene's *Pandosto. The Triumph of Time* (1588) and Lawrence Twine's *The Patterne of Painefull Adventures* (1594) provide useful examples of this use of geographic awareness, for both situate themselves in locations about which early modern readers had substantial knowledge. Within the European world Greene presents or the New Testament associations with the cultures of Twine's romance, both authors insert clearly fictional locations that emphasize the geographic realities the works otherwise inhabit. The texts contain geographic lies, and those falsehoods clarify the central function of geographic truth within Greene's and Twine's texts.

The Trapalonian Gentleman and the Paduan Bride

Greene's *Pandosto* has been one of the early modern romances most closely linked with geographical concerns, if only indirectly, through Shakespeare's use of it as the primary source for *The Winter's Tale*, which has long been noted for the geographic anomaly at its center. The Bohemian seacoast of Shakespeare's play is matched by a similarly fictitious coastline in Greene's romance despite the presence of maps in the 1580s, which clearly showed Bohemia's landlocked nature. The geographical "gaff" of Shakespeare's has been easily dismissible as a simple borrowing from his source in Robert Greene's tale.[1] Josef Polišenský, for instance, asserts that despite England's knowledge of Bohemia, "Bohemia, like Russia and Sicily, came under the heading of far-away dream lands when the genre of the play demanded it"

(197).[2] However, if we are actually examining *Pandosto* itself, no such luxury is permitted us. Although Shakespeare did not borrow the whole of Greene's romance—Greene, for instance, includes no Autolycus figure, no Paulina figure, and most significantly, no statue scene—he does adopt (though he reverses) Greene's geography. And this geography plays a significant role in how we ought to read the romance and how its original audience would have understood the implications of the locations in which the narrative is set.

The text contains only a few geographical markers: Pandosto and his wife, Bellaria, rule Bohemia, which generally remains uncharacterized by descriptive language that smacks of geographically didactic intent (we are introduced to the location simply by the statement: "In the country of Bohemia there reigned a king" [155]).[3] We do learn that Egistus, the visiting king from the equally undescribed Sicilia (or Sicily), whom Pandosto believes is guilty of adultery with his wife, "sailed into Bohemia" (156), confirming for us the geographical "error" of the text. As in *The Winter's Tale*, the infant wrongly believed to be the offspring of an affair between Bellaria and Egistus is cast adrift in a boat that eventually lands on the coast of Sicily. There she grows up as a shepherdess named Fawnia who is eventually prompted to flee across the ocean with the Prince Dorastus for fear of Egistus's reaction to their intended marriage. Their ship is blown to Bohemia, where the Prince lies to Pandosto, claiming that he is a knight from "Trapalonia" fleeing Italy with his Paduan-born bride to escape the displeasure of her family. Eventually their true identities are revealed, and Pandosto accepts their union; it is worth noting that before the revelation of their identities he had imagined himself as Fawnia's husband and had even threatened to rape her (200). The two lovers accompanied by Pandosto return to Sicily, where their wedding is celebrated and where Pandosto subsequently commits suicide in remorse over his prior actions. Dorastus and Fawnia take his corpse and return to rule in Bohemia. There are a few other scattered geographical references: to Russia (163), where Bellaria is from (she is identified as the daughter of the Emperor of Russia); to Delphos (168–69), where Apollo's oracle is received; to Denmark (177), where a marriage is proposed between Dorastus and the king's daughter; and to Italy (188), where Dorastus and Fawnia intend to flee before they are blown off course.

The geographical mapping of the text merits detailed analysis not only because of the creation of a seacoast for Bohemia but also because of the presence of the romance's reference to "Trapalonia": a fictional place. If one fictional location could be created for the purposes of the tale, why not create others, especially if there is going to be no insistence on using these locations accurately? Polišenský studied the links between Bohemia and England during the later part of the sixteenth century and the early seventeenth century, concluding that there were significant contacts between the two countries through traveling English acting companies, Sir Philip Sidney, Fynes Moryson, Elizabeth Jane Weston, John Dee, and Samuel Lewkenor; as well as through Bohemians traveling to England, most notably Peter Fradelius (who traveled to England in 1616) and Zdeněk Brtnický (who came to England in 1600).[4] He concludes that although most information the English had about Bohemia was obtained secondhand, the country was known for its religious toleration and its links to alchemy[5]; however, he concludes that this cultural knowledge about Bohemia really does not matter much to either Greene or Shakespeare, except that Shakespeare needed to set *The Winter's Tale* in "an unreal, fairy-tale Bohemia because only in a fairy tale could the growing conflicts of society be resolved" (201).[6] Perhaps the improbabilities of Shakespeare's play require a fantastic setting, but why a fantastic Bohemia instead of Moscovy or Illyria or America? Certainly Greene's romance, which is less fantastic or improbable (there is no resurrection of the dead queen), needs a fictionalized location less. And if a fictionalized locale is required, why not fill the entire text with geographic fictions? The answer, I think, lies in the clash between what Greene's readers might be expected to know about the cultures represented in *Pandosto* and the obviousness of the creation of the fictional Trapalonia. Given the amount of information sixteenth-century England had about Bohemia and Eastern Europe, the Trapalonian lie becomes glaring, and it challenges readers' conclusions about the surface narrative itself.

Discussions of Bohemia in early modern travel and ethnographic texts tend to emphasize it as an urban center (Prague figures largely in these reports) containing the ills attendant upon that status (crime, ugliness, noxious odors), as well as its advantages (universities, cathedrals, marketplaces). Generally, discussions of Bohemia seem to be folded into discussions of the Holy Roman Empire of Germany. The most common comment made about it seems to be a reference to the role of its king as an elector of the emperor.[7] Abbot's *A Briefe Description of the Whole Worlde* informs us, in addition to that fact, that "Bohemia is a kingdome in the middle of Germanie, which is compassed rounde with a mightie wood, called *Silua Hicimia:* the chiefe citie thereof is called Prage" (sig. Aiiiᵛ).

Samuel Lewkenor's *A Discourse Not Altogether Vnprofitable . . . Containing a Discourse of all those Cities Wherein Do Flourish at this Day Priuiledged Vniuersities* (1600), is a key text for early modern understanding of Bohemia, for it includes a detailed description of Prague during a discussion of the universities of Bohemia and Moravia.[8] Although this postdates Greene's romance, it claims to be largely culled from previous authors and contains a table of authors "whose authorities are alleadged in this worke" (sig. A5ᵛ). Lewkenor is largely adulatory in tone. The "great and renowned citie," in Lewkenor's account, is filled with "many ancient and goodly edifices," marketplaces, and intricately wrought public clocks. He dwells on the city's religious character, describing the legend of St. Vinceslaus and identifying Wycliffe, Jerome of Prague, and John Hus as three of the city's important past residents. He describes the Jewish quarter, in which the Jews "haue their peculiar lawes and liberties" (sig Q2ᵛ). There is no hint of derogation.

One work of the period that discusses Bohemia—admittedly a little later than *Pandosto*'s 1588 publication date—is Moryson's *An Itinerary . . . Conteinying His Ten Yeeres Travell Throvgh The Twelve Dominions of Germany, Bohmerland, Sweiterland, Netherland, Denmarke, Poland, Italy, Turky, France, England, Scotland, and Ireland* (published in 1617, although the travels themselves began in 1591).[9] Moryson describes Bohemia in a few places within his lengthy work. He describes Prague as poorly fortified and filthy. The buildings there he finds are "built with little beauty or Art, the walls being all of whole trees as they come out of the wood, the which with the barke are laid so rudely, as they may on both sides be seen."[10] Most of his further discussion of Bohemia is devoted to its legal system, its mode of government, and its method of taxation. However, he does also report that in Prague

> harlots be there as common as in *Italy*, and dwell in streets together, (where they stand at the doores, and by wanton signes allure passe[n]gers to them) yet I did see some men and women of the common sort, who for simple fornication, were yoked in carts, & therewith drew out of the City the filth of the streets. But while the Bohemians thus chasten the poorer sort, I feare the greater Flies escape their webs. (III. 20[9])

Adultery, however, is punished by death (II. 20), and Bohemians are more "invested with forraigne fashions" than the Germans (III. 169). Moryson also reports that travel in Bohemia is "tedious," largely due to the mountainous terrain and poor road conditions (I. 295); that Bohemian magistrates—like their Italian counterparts—never pardon murderers (II. 26); and that Bohemians will never intercede to break up a quarrel between two men (III. 26). The country is also identified as being "farre within land and hath no great commodities to bee exported" (III. 90). The combined effect of texts such as Lewkenor's and Moryson's is to create a sense of Bohemia as an urban location: it is a place of citified ugliness, of sexuality as commodity, of criminality, and of unpleasant smells.

Sicily, on the other hand, is represented in texts of the period as a site of agricultural abundance set amidst contemporary religious and political turmoil and mythological accommodation to rape. Moryson's text, although it discusses various aspects of Italy as a whole (such as its laws, fashions, architecture, and the layouts of several of its cities), does not specifically describe the island of Sicily, which (like Italy in general) is often during the period associated with Catholicism and superstition. Politically, Sicily was recognized as a volatile location, control of it having been transferred several times between Byzantine, Muslim, and Christian rulers. M. Blundeville's *His Exercises, Containing Sixe Treatises* (1594), a work describing the use of globes, maps, and sextants, as well as explaining arithmetic and astrolabes to a readership of young men, describes Sicily as a place that

> hath bene always famous, and is called of Diodorus the Paragon of Iles, also the Greekes and the Latines haue greatly celebrated this Ile in their writings. This Iland hath great aboundance of Wheat and of al other grain, also of Wine, Sugar, Waxe, Honey, Saffron, Silk, and of all things els appertaining to the vse of man. Wherefore this Ile, togethre with Aegypt was sometime called the Grange of the Romanes.[11]

Other writers, such as George Sandys, also emphasize Sicily's role as classical Rome's grainery, as well as its identification as the setting for the mythological rape of Proserpina.[12]

Against this geographical backdrop, the contrast between the factual locations of Greene's text and the fictional Trapalonia become more striking. Bohemia seems—given what Moryson describes as its ugliness—an appropriate setting for irrational jealousy, unfounded charges of adultery, and (in the next generation) the deceit of the young lovers. Sicily, as a place of fecundity, seems an apt location for harboring the innocent princess whose union with the prince Dorastus will reunite the two fighting dynasties and will provide some hope for an optimistic future as the next generation of rulers weds and prepares to assume its position. But a Sicilian location also casts a darker light to that same marriage, if we see Sicily as the location from which Proserpina was abducted by Pluto and as the original land-scape for the compromise that traps her with her rapist for a substantial portion of each year. Sicily requires female accommodation to patriarchal order in order to maintain its identity as an idyllic pastoral world.

Read through the "glasse" of Moryson and Lewkenor, both Sicily and Bohemia are somewhat threatening spaces. Bohemia is not only a location of urban squalor and illicit sexuality but a location of laws and punishments as well. In this framework, it is a fitting place to threaten the union of the two lovers (and in Bohemia Pandosto threatens not only Fawnia with rape, but Fawnia, her foster father, and Dorastus's servant with execution as well). The inappropriateness of performing their marriage in that culture is clear. Under Pandosto's command it is not a culture that nurtures the kind of seemingly class-defying love that binds the two characters; it is not a cul-ture that is equipped to encourage the possibility of fecundity and natural growth, even tempered by the accommodation that the tale of Proserpina implies, that they have been able to find on Sicily. And the sordidness of the location certainly combines with the moral taint of its king to make it an inappropriate setting for a joyful marriage. Returning to Sicily for the mar-riage itself, then, is only *more* appropriate than a marriage in Bohemia: Sic-ily is not an idyllic site. Pandosto's inclusion in the group traveling to Sicily emphasizes this point by further injecting a sexually sinister note into that landscape. He brings from Bohemia not only the stigma of its urban licen-tiousness but also that of his own contemplated rape of his daughter and his later suicide there. The return of the young couple to rule in Bohemia at the close of the text may suggest the communal renewal typically found at the close of comedies and romances, but it also suggests that the kind of pastoral fantasy in which Dorastus and Fawnia engaged in Sicily is only that—a temporary respite from the modern realities of life in a culture such as Bohemia. Furthermore, even its idyllic quality is undercut by the violent sexuality implied by both its links to the rape of Proserpina and the intro-duction into it of the would-be rapist, Pandosto.[13] Greene marks the miti-gated quality of the romance's conclusion by the final clauses of his last sentence: "Dorastus, taking leave of his father, went with his wife and the dead corpse [of Pandosto] into Bohemia where, after they were sumptuously

entombed, Dorastus ended his days in contented quiet" (204). The conclusion shifts our attention back to Bohemia, to the grimness of Pandosto's
error, and, perhaps most significantly, away from Fawnia.[14]

This point bears special emphasis: the narrative has generally prompted
us to believe that it is Fawnia whose growth and progress are to be central
to our experience of the text. Yet, she becomes elided from the conclusion—raped and hidden away as Proserpina was?—so that readers are left
to believe that closure comes not from her narrative, from her return to the
place of her birth, but from Dorastus's return to govern it. From the impo-
sition of Sicilian values and the presence of a reassuringly patriarchal ruler
emerges a remote hope that Bohemia can become something of the nur-
turing place Sicily was. Recognizing the culture's associations with and
knowledge of both Bohemia and Sicily permits us to understand more fully
the cultural likelihood of the presence of moral problems in Bohemia as
well as the need to flee Sicily. It helps us to understand further the embedded allusions to rape and the representations of gender relations implied by
the shift in focus at the narrative's end from Fawnia as the abandoned princess to Dorastus as the new Bohemian ruler. It helps us to see that the
resolution the romance provides really furnishes us with less closure, with
less optimism, than we might initially suspect.

The geographic lie of Trapalonia stands in stark contrast to the vaguely
sinister implications of the texts' factual geographic spaces.[15] This place is
clearly marked for us as a geographic anomaly by Pandosto's response to
Dorastus's claim to be a "Trapalonian gentleman"—he reacts "as one in cho-
ler" and promptly assumes that Dorastus's "smooth tale hath but small truth"
(196). Pandosto immediately recognizes the fictionality of Trapalonia, and
the attempt of the young lovers to deceive him geographically is what will
not be tolerated. It is intolerable because it suggests the possibility of a utopian location removed from the corruption, both political and sexual, present
in both Bohemia and Sicily. There can be no ideal in this romance, as Pandosto
well knows from his previous seemingly motiveless destruction of his own
marriage, and he rejects Dorastus's attempts to construct such a fiction.

The geographic lie is also significant in gendered terms as well. The disguised Dorastus claims that he is from Trapalonia; he claims Fawnia, however, to be from Padua. Although his representing Fawnia as from an actual
geographic location could be interpreted as an attempt to assert Dorastus's
honorable nature, because he thereby shields her from the charge of geo-

graphical lying, it also prevents her from participating in the utopian fantasy that Trapalonia implies. She is prevented from being removed, even discursively, from the complex associations surrounding Italian geography.[16] Fawnia, while elided from the text's final sentence and from ruling Bohemia, as we have previously seen, is not permitted geographic isolation. She may not be removed from a geographic space to be inserted into a de Certeauian fictional "place." She remains geographically fixed despite her disguise, suggesting the difficulty of true disguises for female characters: they may not hide from the implications of geography.

The Spaces and Places of Painful Adventures

The intimate linkage between geography, gender, and fictional narrative that is present in *Pandosto* is made clear by the attempt to violate geographic fact. Fictionalizing Bohemia and inventing Trapalonia prevents readers from experiencing *Pandosto* wholly as either ethnography or as satisfying fantasy. The geographic limits of its world create the limits of its fictionality, and similarly link those limits to its female heroine. Lawrence Twine's *The Patterne of Painefull Adventures* (1594) creates a similar kind of geographic fictionality that qualifies its ethnographic and romance value. Like *Pandosto* its geography has received a fair amount of indirect scholarly attention because of the romance's role as a primary source for Shakespeare's *Pericles*. Shakespeare borrows all of the locations Twine used, with two significant exceptions: instead of having his young heroine sold into a brothel in Mytilene, as Shakespeare does, Twine's analogous character is found in "Machilenta," where she discusses another culture Shakespeare drops, the "Lapsatenians."[17] As in *Pandosto*, fictional geography is created at the moment of the sexual maturation of the romance's heroine. Like Greene's romance, Twine's retreat from geographic reality undermines the resolution of the romance and emphasizes the ethnographic realities the text otherwise implies.

Near the end of Twine's romance we learn that its main character, Apollonius, in his old age

> applied his vacant time to his booke, and hee wrote the whole storie and discourse of his owne life and adventures at large, the which he caused to be written foorth in two large volumes, whereof he sent

one to the Temple of Diana at Ephesus, and placed the other in his owne library. Of which historie this is but a small abstract, promising if ever the whole chance to come into my hands, to set it forth with all fidelitie, diligence, and expedition. (481)[18]

This moment in the text is noteworthy because it provides an unexpectedly clear appeal to history and exemplarity in the work. Although our narrator has occasionally intruded into the text, he has given no overt indication that we should expect to find such an appeal, an appeal much more typical in the prefaces of the period. Thomas Lodge's *A Margarite of America* (1596), for instance, provides its readers with a preface that informs us that Lodge

som foure yeres being at sea with M. *Candish* (whose memorie if I repent not, I lament not) it was my chance in the librarie of the Jesuits in *Sanctum* to find this historie in the Spanish tong, which as I read delighted me, and delighting me, wonne me, and winning me made me write it.[19]

Lodge permits the "historie" some fictionalized status (its representation of some kind of historical "truth" in the Spanish version is not discussed), but in its English version the story gains an aura of authenticity, of veracity from the fable of its origin among the Jesuits in Spain. And certainly, identifying the author as translator and not originator removes him from full responsibility for the narrative he is about to present. By contrast, Twine's prefatory letter to Master John Donning contains no fictionalized authorizations for the text as history, or to the legendary status of the story of Apollonius of Tyre. The only early appeal to a historical truth for the romance comes in the first line of the opening chapter, which echoes the conventional novella opening:

The most famous and mightie king Antiochus, which builded the goodly citie of Antiochia in Syria, and called it after his own name, as the chiefest seate of all his dominions, and most principal place of his abode, begat upon his wife one daughter, a most excellent and beautifull yoong Ladie. (426)

In other words, as is true at the beginning of so many early modern fictions, at this opening moment of the text, it is through an appeal to place that Twine's narrative finds itself anchored to an appeal to a historical past, to a representational "truth." The later appeal to historical truth is also an appeal to the kind of factuality contained in travel and ethnographic texts of the period. Despite Twine's deferring our awareness of the role of travel literature in authorizing his text, geography plays a significant role in his romance, as it does in Shakespeare's version of the tale.[20]

An important observation from which to begin a discussion of Twine's ethnographic dimension is that his text is divided into chapters of which two-thirds explicitly name the country that is central to their narrative action. In other words, the text seems structured to call our attention to the places it represents. This is certainly fitting, of course, in a Heliodoran romance about "painefull adventures." As with Sidney's *Arcadia* or Greene's *Pandosto*, geographic spaces are integral to the romance's action and meaning. Twine's world is significant too because of its emphasis on creating spaces not through didactic description of customs or natural history, but through an emphasis on the civic dimension of the locations in which it is set. Early in the romance Twine presents the incest between Antiochus and his daughter not as consensual but as rape; moreover, it is not represented merely as a private transgression but as a public crime within a civic context. Although the daughter laments to her nurse the loss of her virginity, her father "sheweth the countenance of a loving sire abroad in the eies of his people" (427). This brief reference to the public world in which these characters operate is echoed repeatedly in Twine's narrative. In the following chapter, when Apollonius flees Tyre to escape the murderers sent by Antiochus, the narrator reports,

The day following, his subjects the citizens came unto the Pallace to have seene their Prince, but when they found him not there, the whole citie was forthwith surprised with wonderfull sorrowe, everie man lamenting that so worthy a Prince [was] so sodainly gone out of sight and knowledge, no man knew whether. Great was the grief, and wofull was the wayling which they made, every man lamenting his owne private estate and the commonwealths in generall, as it alwaies hapneth at the death or losse of a good Prince, which the inhabitants of Tirus tooke then so heavily, in respect of their great affection, that a long time after no barbers shops were opened, the common shews and plaies surceased, baines and hoat houses were shut up, taverns were not frequented, and no man repaired unto the Churches, al thing was

full of sorrow and heaviness, what shall I say? There was nothing but
heavinesse. (430–31)

The whole city responds to Apollonius's loss. The early episodes in
Tharsus, in which Apollonius relieves the city's famine, are studded with
references to the citizenry, their consent to accept Apollonius's help (432),
and the first of several speeches he will make to the citizens of the places he
visits. In Pentapolis, the king, Altistrates, announces his daughter's engagement to Apollonius to the "nobliest of his subjects and frends out of the
confederat cities and countries" (443); in Tharsus, the dying nurse tells
Tharsia that should her foster parents threaten her she should defend herself by running to the statue of her father in the marketplace "saying: O
Citizens of Tharsus, I am his daughter, whose image this is: and the citizens
being mindfull of thy fathers benefites, will doubtlesse revenge thine injurie"
(453); the statue to the presumed dead Tharsia is dedicated in Tharsus with
a speech to "dearly beloved friendes and Citizens of Tharsus" (455). In the
final chapters of the narrative, the citizens of Machilenta are consulted about
how to punish the bawd who enslaved Tharsia ("My lorde Apollonius, we
judge that he be burned alive, and his goods be given unto the maiden
Tharsia" [469]), Apollonius delivers a farewell address to them, and they
decide to erect statues to Apollonius and Tharsia. Apollonius (backed by an
army) later addresses the citizens of Tharsus and stirs them to avenge the
attempted murder of his daughter (476). Even the pirates (another kind of
"citizen"?) who had abducted Tharsia and thus prevented her murder return at the close of the narrative; they are thanked for their serendipitous
protection of Tharsia and knighted because Apollonius "knew that the sinister means which they hitherto had insued was caused most by constraint,
for want of other trade or abilitie to live by" (480). The *Painefull Adventures*,
in other words, makes the places in which the story occurs locations in
which people live, in which courts and pastoral retreats are not the only
dwellings to be found. Moreover, the characters who occupy these locations are significant figures who are to be consulted about matters concern-
ing their communities.

The recuperation of the pirates at the narrative's close raises an economic dimension to the representation of place within the text. As Apollonius quickly ascribes their behavior to economic need and lack of voca-
tional training, other points within the text also echo a language of
economics and trade. Specifically, Twine's narrative seems to invoke the

language of the merchant adventurer whose reports are contained in works such as Hakluyt's *Principal Navigations* or Purchas's *Purchas His Pilgrimes*. For example, Apollonius's relieving the famine of Tharsus early in the narrative is cast as an economic transaction. Apollonius offers the city "an hundred thousand bushels of wheate, paying no more than I bought it for in mine owne countrey, that is to say, eight peeces of brasse for everie bushell" (432). Despite the fact that it is Apollonius who establishes the terms of the economic exchange, he subsequently rejects the deal he had proposed:

> But Apollonius, doubting lest by this deede he should seeme to put off the dignitie of a prince, and put on the countenance of a merchant rather than a giver, when he had received the price of the wheate, he restored it backe againe to the use and commoditie of the same citie." (433)

Apollonius fears constructing himself as a merchant driven by economic motives rather than aristocratic noblesse oblige. He rejects identification with someone like Sebastian Cabot, who, in his "Ordinances for the direction of the intended voyage for Cathay" (1553), describes how merchant travelers may lure indigenous peoples to examine the "commodities" they carry for sale and states that

> the names of the people of every island, are to be taken in writing, with the commodities of the same, their natures, qualities, and dispositions, what commodities they will most willingly depart with, and what metals they have in hills, mountains, streams, or rivers, in, or under the earth.[21]

Twine seems to want to construct his text to echo elements of the merchant traveler's report while having his main character reject full identification with the writers of such texts. Nonetheless, the text repeatedly invokes merchandising language. Apollonius's departure from Tyre is couched in the behavior of the merchant (as he loads his ships up with grain, gold, silver, and "rich apparell" [429]); Apollonius becomes merchandise himself as Antiochus offers 100 talents of gold for the capture of Apollonius alive and 50 for returning his dead body to the king (431). Later, he figures his relationship to economic exchange more ambiguously. Entrusting his infant daughter to Stranguilio and Dionisiades, Apollonius states,

For I will not returne backe againe unto king Altistrates my father-in-law, whose daughter alas, I have lost in the sea, but meaning rather to excercise the trade of merchandize, I commit my daughter unto you. (451)

How are we to read this? Has he exchanged his daughter for the life of a merchant? Was his wife similarly seen as a piece of merchandise lost at sea? The life of a trader, however, seems to become irrelevant here, for after he leaves Tharsia in Tharsus, we learn that he "departed unto his ship, and sailed into far countries, and unto the uppermost parts of Egypt" (451), but no mention is made of the business he conducts there. We do later learn while he is recounting his adventures in the Temple of Diana at Ephesus that Apollonius seems to have spent all of the fourteen years of his mourning period in the "higher partes of Egypt" (472), a location linked not only to Cleopatra but also to the more civilized aspects of African "barbarity." It was also, as we have observed in relation to Sidney's story of Plangus and Erona, a location linked to Islam, to the Turks, to learning in mathematics and astronomy, to justice, and to superstition,[22] but sending Apollonius to Egypt—either as merchant or mourner—is a way of sending him out of the civilized world to mark his departure from court life and Western "civility," to insert him into the prosaic world of Hakluyt's merchant explorers. The connections the romance makes between travel texts and its narrative move Apolonius into the realm of cultural Otherness, much as we have observed occurring in novellas that include contact with the East, such as Painter's tale of "Amadour and Florinda." Apollonius becomes enmeshed in the non-European associations that Egypt suggests and the nonromantic associations of economic merchant discourse, a link that continues in Twine's romance as the text moves to the episode in which Apollonius's daughter Tharsia becomes an object of obvious economic value when she is sold into slavery and then bid on as a prostitute.

The selling of Tharsia, of course, provides the central image of economic exchange in the narrative. Twine has his readers eavesdrop on a bidding war that occurs between the bawd and Athanagoras, the governor of Machilenta and analogue for Shakespeare's Lysimachus. In Twine's version, this character is not just someone who visits the orphaned captive in the brothel. He attempts to "out-bid the bawd," but ultimately stops bidding because "if I should contend with the bawd to buy her at so hie a price, I must needes sell other slaves to pay for her, which were both losse and shame unto me" (456). His motives are driven by economics and driven too by his sense of civic responsibility. He then intends to be her first customer. As in *Pericles,* she persuades him not to rape her and she receives a greater payment from him than had been set for her virginity. Athanagoras himself eavesdrops while she entertains her second customer in the same manner and receives an even greater payment from him. The narrative at this point assumes the quality of a jest book as the two frustrated johns

> sware an othe betweene themselves, that they would not bewray those words [that she had spoken to persuade them not to deflower her] unto any, & they withdrew themselves aside into a secret place, to see the going in and comming foorth of other, and they sawe many which went in and gave their mony, and came foorth againe weeping. (458)

This pattern of behavior continues until Tharsia insists on being brought "into the marketplace of the citie" (459) so she can earn money by displaying her skills and her learning. She continues to be a focus of economics when, after Apollonius has arrived at Machilenta, she earns one hundred gold pieces from Apollonius for leaving him after having entertained him with a riddle, and two hundred from Athanagoras for returning to tell him some more. Not only does she become the object of economic exchange, but she takes control of her own merchandising, subverting the typical romance position of virgin daughters as objects of exchange struggling under strict patriarchal control, such as we have seen in the case of *Pandosto's* Fawnia or, we might argue, in any early modern literary example of father-daughter incest. As Brenda Cantar has observed in relation to Greene's *Pandosto* and *Menaphon:*

> In the cultural contexts of these romances, daughters—like their mothers—were most highly valued for their reproductive potential: marriage to the appropriate partner served to revivify and perpetuate the structure of family and society. . . . Yet such claustrophobic vigilance seeks to establish a situation whereby a daughter's sexuality excites a variety of ambivalent emotions manifested in her father's arbitrary and violently incestuous desire.[23]

The literal incest of Pandosto or Antiochus becomes projected onto economics in the case of Apollonius in Machilenta. Although he expresses no sexual desire for Tharsia, he pays her, like those men who had, one hundred gold pieces to leave him to his grief (464). Athanagoras promptly offers her two hundred more to return to Apollonius and provoke him to abandon his mourning. She is not the disguised romance heroine like Fawnia at this point; she is an economic working woman wresting control of her own subjectivity away from patriarchal forces.

The link between royalty and the merchant adventurer that her father establishes for himself early in the narrative becomes transferred to Tharsia. Certainly, her position in a brothel necessitates that she be seen in economic terms—regardless of the genre—but the links that the prose text establishes to narratives of travel and trade imbue her economic position with vitality. She becomes the subject of jest and economic competition in three separate scenes (her purchasing, her "deflowering," her riddling with her unknown father), and this economic focus is authorized, at least in part, by the connections made between her narrative and the place in which it occurs.

Twine locates these events in the geographically fictional "Machilenta," a place he leaves undescribed except to report that the pirates who had captured Tharsia "by benefite of happie winde arrived at Machilenta, and came into the citie" (455).[24] Moreover, during an argument with a bawd Tharsia has soon after her arrival there, she gestures toward a statue of Priapus and says: "God forbid master, that I should worship such an idoll. But (sir) said she, are you a Lapsatenian? Why askest thou? said the bawd[.] I aske, quoth she, because the Lapsatenians doe worship Priapus" (456). Like Machilenta, the Lapsatenians are fictional. Twine retreats to fictional geography and ethnography for the setting of the economically and subjectively active Tharsia—and by locating her in fictional places rather than in geographic spaces, he makes her subjectivity safely fictional.

The fictionality of Machilenta and the Lapsatenians is supplemented by another geographic factor: the naming of Apollonius's daughter. In Twine's romance, her name, Tharsia, is drawn from Tharsus, the city in which she is first nurtured as an infant and then threatened when she reaches maturity. By naming her after Tharsus, Twine links her to her father's succoring of its people, an act aligned with both aristocratic magnanimity and the economics of the merchant traveler. She becomes metonymically linked to Tharsus and its people (a people, it should be remembered, who will rise up to effect justice for her attempted murder), and Tharsus is clearly associated with the travels of the apostle Paul. In fact, the geographic locations that the romance names might be expected to evoke rapid identification by its early modern readers because the 1560 Geneva Bible included a map of Paul's travels that identifies the other locations that Twine's text names.[25] In addition, other current references would link these locations with the Ottoman Turks.[26] In other words, Tharsia becomes linked by her name with geographic realities that problematize her relationship to the Christian West just as her imprisonment in a fictional location draws attention to the impossibility of the threat to patriarchal control that her exercise of economic subjectivity suggests.

Like Greene, Twine also uses fictional locations to isolate his female character and to limit her subjectivity. The sexual and economic independence that Tharsia shows is safely placed in the fictional Machilenta, removed from the world that travelers and ethnographers have described for Twine's readers: the anxiety Tharsia causes is safely removed from them. Similarly, the refusal to permit Fawnia the same fictional freedom allays anxieties about female sexual and political power as well—fictional places isolate and contain cultural threats much more readily than do cultures accessible by the "glasse" of observation and report.

5

The Ethnographic Function of Latin

CLOUDING THE "GLASSE" FOR WOMEN READERS

What occurs in *Pandosto* and *The Patterne of Painefull Adventures* is that the ethnographic dimension becomes so taken for granted that shifts into fictional geography mark shocking textual moments. In fact, the ethnographic impulse we have been examining becomes so embedded in the texts themselves that it seems to take many forms. For example, consider this additional passage from Twine's text, taken from its early pages. A boy, clad only with a towel around "his middle" runs through the streets of Pentapolis calling out, "Whosoever will be washed, let him come to the place of exercise" (435). Apollonius follows the boy and

> comming unto the place cast off his cloake, and stripped himselfe, and entred the Baine, and bathed himselfe with the liquor. And looking about for some companion with whome he might exercise himself according unto the manner of the place and countrey, and finding none: sodainelie unlooked for entred in Altistrates King of the whole land, accompanied with a great troupe of servitours. Anone he beganne to exercise himself at tennis with his men, which when Apolonius espied, he intruded himselfe amongst them into the kings presence, and stroke back the ball to the king, and served him in play with great swiftnes. But when the king perceived the great nimblenesse and cunning which was in him, surpassing the residue: stand aside (quoth he) unto his men, for

me thinkes this yong man is more cunning than I. When Apollonius heard himselfe commended, hee stept foorth boldly into the middes of the tennis court, and taking up a racket in his hand, he tossed the ball skilfully, and with wonderful agilitie. After play, he also washed the king very reverently in the Baine: and when all was done, hee tooke his leave duetifully, & so departed. When Apollonius was gone, the king said unto them that were about him: I sweare unto you of truth as I am a Prince, I was never exercised nor washed better then this day, and that by the diligence of a yong man I know not what he is. (435–56)

Notice how the king wishes to "exercise himself according unto the manner of the place and countrey." The text invites its readers to see the voyeuristic, erotic passage that follows as a kind of gloss upon that phrase. We have previously been informed that the city we are in is Pentapolis, but this passage encourages us to understand that such homosocial play is common in Pentapolis. The ethnographic dimension of the passage is clear, yet it is subordinated to the more overt eroticism of the scene.

The assimilation of the ethnographic in early fiction takes other forms as well. Not only may descriptions of spaces and activities occurring within them function as ethnographic "glasses," but so may the language by which such locations and activities are presented. In particular, the humanist discourse that emphasized education in Latin and the classics as a means of achieving a gentlemanly education created a tendency to read fiction didactically, as if it were part of the program of humanist education. This tendency is best exemplified by two different kinds of fictional strategies—the use of Latin within texts and the use of texts as a means of amplifying the educational material found in classical texts, most notably Ciceronian texts, to suggest that the status of the fictional texts was the equivalent of that provided by nonfictional Latin discourse. The most notable example of how these two complementary impulses converged in the construction of early fiction is found in Robert Greene's *Ciceronis Amor: Tullies Love* (1589), which claims to fill in gaps in the Elizabethan reader's knowledge of Cicero's life by describing his courtship of his wife, Terentia, while simultaneously employing Latin within the text to augment that informative goal.[1]

Although Greene's text will provide the primary focus of my discussion here, it is not alone in its use of Latin or its attempt to align itself with the nonfictional discourse of humanist educational treatises and practices. Like ethnographic and travel literature, humanist texts, like Thomas Elyot's *Book of the Governour* and Roger Ascham's *The Schoolmaster,* provide a reading environment that claims to be morally didactic and edifying. And like these texts, early modern fiction establishes some of the same claims for the same purposes—to establish the texts as not being a waste of time, but as providing their readers with an education about the world outside their English experience. Ascham, for instance, describes his final visit with Lady Jane Grey:

> Her parents, the duke and duchess, with all the household, gentlemen and gentlewomen, were hunting in the park. I found her in her chamber, reading *Phaedon Platonis* in Greek, and that with as much delight as some gentleman would read a merry tale in Boccace. After salutation and duty done, with some other talk, I asked her why she would leese such pastime in the park[.] Smiling, she answered me, "Iwis, all their sport in the park is but a shadow to that pleasure I find in Plato! Alas good folk, they never felt what true pleasure meant."[2]

His elation at seeing her reading Plato with as much pleasure as others might read the *Decameron* is balanced by his more explicit criticism for Italian works of fiction:

> And yet ten *Morte Darthurs* do not the tenth part so much harm as one of these books made in Italy and translated in England. They open, not fond and common ways to vice, but such subtle, cunning, new, and diverse shifts to carry young wills to vanity and young wits to mischief, to teach old bawds new school-points, as the simple head of an Englishman is not hable to invent, nor never was hard of in England before, yea, when papistry overflowed all. Suffer these books to be read, and they shall soon displace all books of godly learning.[3]

For Ascham, reading fiction is a risky business that the humanistically educated individual must guard against, but Plato is to be read with the pleasure that is normally accorded the reading of fiction. The boundaries—at least in the effects of the works—have blurred. As R. W. Maslen phrases it in his lucid discussion of Ascham's reaction to Italianate fiction, Ascham feared that such fictions would "occupy the same territory as pedagogic treatises."[4] An interesting geographic image, even from the remove of our distant perspective. Fictions such as the *Decameron* and the novella collections it spawned create the impression of providing didactic material, as we have seen. Prose romances function similarly, and the education they provide is not just geographic, but it is linguistic, biographical, and historical as well.

The linguistic dimension of its educative value should not be underestimated. In Shakespeare's *Merchant of Venice,* a text that includes a short course in Elizabethan ethnic biases, we learn of Portia's English suitor that he "hath neither Latin, French, nor Italian. . . . He is a proper man's picture, but alas, who can converse with a dumb show?" (1.2.67–71).[5] Perhaps this characterization ought be put alongside Ben Jonson's characterization of Shakespeare as someone with "small Latin, and less Greek," for it suggests that however broadly based the ideal of humanist education Ascham advocated, large segments of the English population, even among the upper classes, remained largely untrained in Latin. This point is eloquently emphasized by John Hale, who observes that during the Renaissance Latin "had always been a learned patina on the intarsia of vernaculars and this was wearing thinner than ever,"[6] which is emphasized by much of the fiction from the period. *Lazarillo de Tormes* (1554; trans. 1586) includes, for example, a vignette about a seller of indulgences who manipulates the priests he tricks through their knowledge of Latin:

> He found out how well educated they were. If they said they knew Latin then he never said a word in that language so as not to put his foot in it. . . . If he found out that the clergy were just reverends and, because they had more money than education, had been ordained without following a proper course, then you'd think he was St. Thomas Aquinas. He would talk in Latin for two hours. Of course it wasn't Latin but it did sound like it.[7]

Latin represented a kind of knowledge that was both desirable and increasingly superficial, even among those whose training was supposed to include it. And as more individuals obtained only "small Latin," fictional texts became a place where the veneer of humanist education and Latin training could be maintained and, through the use of that veneer, the implications of its value critiqued. Fiction became a discourse that could fill the gap between the real level of learning and the actual level of knowledge, much as it did the kinds of geographic and ethnographic gaps we have already seen it try to fill. A wide range of fictional texts include Latin, including such varied works as George Pettie's *Petite Palace of Pettie His Pleasure*

(1576), which contains specific appeals to female readers; Barnabe Riche's *Don Simonides* (1581–84), which is addressed to both male and female readers; Thomas Nashe's *Unfortunate Traveller* (1594), directed to "Dapper Monsieur Pages of the Court"; Middleton's *Chinon of England* (1597), which makes no claim to having female readers; and Robert Kittowe's *Loues Load-starre* (1600).[8]

The scholarly community has long held that women of various classes were a significant audience for much of the fiction produced during the period. The assumption is so thoroughly established some believe it hardly needs proof. For example, Stephen Orgel simply asserts in a discussion of the possible appeal of the cross-dressing episode in the *Arcadia* to a male readership: "Since the readership of romances was overwhelmingly female—Sidney's title is, after all, *The Countess of Pembroke's Arcadia*—this would, at the very least, constitute a large miscalculation" (80). Juliet Fleming, in a generally informative analysis of the problematic effects of the ways in which works by Pettie and Riche imagine a female audience, reminds us that women had been the imagined audience for prose fiction in Europe from as early as Boccaccio's *Decameron,* which suggests that the tales it contains "should much rather be offered to the charming ladies than to the men" (qtd. Fleming 159). Barnabe Riche's prefatory letter to soldiers accompanying his *Farewell to Militarie Profession* (1581) expresses the hope that his collection "shall please gentlewomen, and that is all the gain that I look for" (128), and a diverse range of works also direct themselves specifically to the attention of female readers.[9] Greene seems to have followed this fashion as well, appealing to female readers so much that he is the likely writer referred to in Thomas Nashe's *The Anatomy of Absurditie* (1589) as "the Homer of women" (1:12).[10] Although Lori Humphrey Newcomb has demonstrated that scholars must be extremely cautious in their conclusions about the appeal of Greene's romances to nonaristocratic women, especially early in their reception history, the fact remains that in the popular mind of much of the culture, romances, in both prose and verse, were associated with a female audience of varying economic and social levels. A description of a chambermaid included in the 1615 edition of Overbury's *Characters* maintains: "She reads *Greenes* works over and over" (qtd. in Newcomb 127).[11] However much ongoing research may want to qualify our sense of who the actual readers of Elizabethan fiction were (and Fleming's work is itself highly instructive on the ways in which appeals to women readers may be used to establish the credibility of a fictional text with male readers[12]), we cannot ignore the prominence of women as constitutive of the imagined majority of the audience for much fictional discourse. And within that imagined framework, the presence of Latin requires much more thorough analysis than it has been given. Certainly Latin was a living language in the predominantly male worlds of the legal system, the university, the church, and the court. Certainly the use of Latin adages was relatively common to much writing of the period. But Elizabethan fiction often goes well beyond simple *aliquid salis* insertions. Greene's *Ciceronis Amor* provides a substantial example of the ways in which the use of Latin functions as a kind of ethnographic "glasse," exposing, much as more obviously geographically didactic fictions do, the complex relationship between humanist ideologies, didacticism, and ideologies of gender in the period. Additional brief examples from works that precede the *Ciceronis Amor* will further demonstrate the scope of the intellectual negotiation current in the period between humanism and female readers of romance.

Grange, Lyly, and Women's Reading of Latin

John Grange's *The Golden Aphroditis* (1577) is a classically inspired narrative about the courtship of the lovers A. O. and N. O. Arthur Kinney has asserted that through its mystical overtones it "aligns itself with the instructive tradition of humanist poetics" (215). It is replete with classical allusions and Latin proverbial phrases (often from Cicero and Terence) that remain untranslated, and it is prefaced by a dedicatory poem addressed to "Courtelike Dames and Ladie-like Gentlewomen" (sig. Bii). The text also includes direct addresses to those female readers at various points throughout the text, sometimes inviting them to try their hand at interpreting the actions of the text's characters. Moreover it contains a striking use of untranslated Latin verse. A spurned lover, to describe his reaction to rejection, sends A. O. a poem containing the following stanzas:

Perhappes *dan Phoebus* in the day, *Minippus* else by night,
In sight, whiche passe *Linceus* eyes, will spie thee forth at length,
With be[n]ding eyes from sun & Moone, who rauisht with thy sight,
In heave[n] wil place thee as a star, none can withsta[n]d their strength.
Thus thou dispising mortall men, the Goddes enioyes at length.

Mitto tibi fro[n]tem Veneris, mediumque Dianae,
Principium lucis quod mare claudet item.
Tempus erit quo tu quia nunc excludis ama[n]tes
Frigidia diserte nocte iacebis anus.

This token herein closed I sende as for my last farewel,
Tis Eglantine, which plainly shews where sweete there soure lay.
My love at first (most like the leaves) did give a fragrant smell.
But now at last, tis like the prickes most hurtful bearing sway.
Yet as the prickes do yeelde no hurt,
Unless some one abuse the smell: (sig. Eiv)

The Latin stanza is set in larger Roman type in the original, distinguishing it from the surrounding black letter and italic type as a kind of emblem or artifact. Reading the Latin stanza and the verse epistle more broadly, A. O.'s anger is "pricked not a little," and she is "set ouer the shoes in dumpes" (sig. Eii). A. O. clearly understands the insult the Latin contains—she seems elsewhere in the text to quote Terence in translation, but what of Grange's female readers? They are left, perhaps, to rely on only a general sense of its implications; the puns surrounding *anus*—which in addition to its primary meaning of "old woman" or "old maid" could mean "ring," with its attendant suggestions of the vagina and anus—are closed off to them. The majority of Grange's female readers are kept from fully experiencing his text— they are placed in a position analogous to that of the aloof A. O. whom the poem ridicules, and the male readers have the value of their Latin education reaffirmed. No attempt is made in this instance to augment the female readers' knowledge of humanist culture or cultural difference; the text remains closed to them, an emblem of their insufficient learning and of the limits of their knowledge. In fact, the text provides a further example of its closure to female readers: throughout the text, snippets of texts by Cicero and Terence are spoken by both N. O. and A. O.; however, only the male character N. O. is permitted to quote them in Latin. A. O.'s quotations are all presented only in translation.

John Lyly's *Euphues and His England* (1580) also attempts to appeal to a female readership (though the first part of *Euphues* did not), and like Grange's text, it limits that appeal through its use of Latin. It contains a dedicatory epistle to "the ladies and gentlemen of England" (2:8) in which he urges women to "take paines to read [his text], . . . *Euphues* had rather lye shut in a Ladyes casket, then open in a Schollers studie" (2:8–9). In general, Lyly seems to construct his text so that it is readable by women; unlike *The Golden Aphroditis,* it contains no scattered Latin phrases to stymie the unhumanistically educated reader. However, late in the text, appended to a section Lyly titles "Euphues Glass for Europe," Lyly presents a thirty-nine-line Latin poem, "Iovis Elizabeth," which describes a contest for supremacy among Athena, Juno, Venus, and Queen Elizabeth. The poem is preceded by an exhortation to European women to imitate the virtues of English women and to pray for their queen, "sith you can neyther sufficiently meruaile at hir, nor I prayse hir" (2:216). Women readers might be able to marvel more fully at the Queen were the poem describing the admiration that the three chief classical goddesses have for her presented to them in English. As in Grange's text, Latin again seems to be used emblematically to signal the inability of female readers to participate fully in the narrative level of the fiction, and thus the use of Latin calls into question the relationship between humanism, didacticism, prevailing ideologies of gender, and the audience of Elizabethan fiction. Grange and Lyly, through their failure to include didactic markers (such as translations of the Latin they include) suggest some measure of confidence in the humanist system, its comprehensiveness, and the appropriateness of excluding women from the full implications their Latin contains. This confidence is further emphasized in Lyly through euphuism itself, with its lists of similitudes drawn from Pliny, Plutarch, Ovid, and other classical figures on whom humanist education relied. But such confidence is offset by other examples of fictional discourse during the period that transform themselves into didactic texts by translating and unpacking the implications of the Latin they contain. For Grange and Lyly, Latin is more clearly a humanist, exclusionary rhetorical strategy; other texts, such as Greene's *Ciceronis Amor,* reveal a more complex relationship, an indication—whether conscious or not— of the collapse of humanist learning as a means of clarifying class and gender relations even as it emphasizes the role of fiction in providing access to a measure of humanist learning.

Other prose texts from the period also highlight the conflicted attitude toward humanist learning that I am trying to describe through their use of both translated and untranslated Latin. *Tarletons News Out of Purgatorie* (1590), for example, contains examples of untranslated Latin, as do John Dickenson's *Arisbas* (1594) and Robert Parry's *Moderatus* (1595), which, following a fairly common pattern, contains untranslated Latin in its prefaces and dedicatory poems, since they are addressed to male readers. Brian Melbancke's

Philotimus (1582) makes its role as humanist text even more explicit, not only by containing untranslated Latin but also by explaining that any obscure vocabulary the text contains is derived from Chaucer or Lydgate or is translated out of Greek or Latin (6). Moreover, *Philotimus* also contains an instance in which an untranslated Latin adage is addressed to a female character who is unable to interpret its meaning or the implications of the letter to which it is appended:

> Amor qui prior, eo potior debet esse.
> When Aurelia se, that neither ye wile of faire words, nor ye reuile of foule writs, could intrept or let his letters, the[n] as one reading a riddle, or constring an Embleame, she stood in a mamering what mean to make, or how to thwart ye cost to shu[n] his gu[n]shot. (Melbancke 125)

The Latin leaves her "mamering," hardly the effect one would be striving for in a letter like this one, trying to persuade the recipient of its writer's love.[13]

The size of the female population possessing the literacy skills necessary to enable the reading of romances is, of course, difficult to answer. David Cressy acknowledges that there were a few women during the period "whose literacy was a social ornament," but he describes the majority of women during the time as "massively illiterate" (128, 106). Probably more women than Cressy admits were taught a basic level of reading competence. As Amy Louise Erickson's research has shown, "Contemporary comment, educational tracts and clerics' diaries confirm that it was not uncommon to teach girls to read along with their brothers, at age 4 or 5"(57). Documentary evidence about the number of women able to read English is sketchy because, as is widely known, even if girls were taught to read—either at home or in petty or dame schools—they were generally removed from school before they were taught to write. Estimating the number of girls whose education extended beyond rudimentary training in English and domestic skills to include a thorough humanist education and, in particular, the Latin instruction such an education presumed, is even more difficult.

Despite the difficulty of determining rates of female Latin literacy during the sixteenth century, the issue is significant to our understanding of Elizabethan prose fiction and its relation to a female readership because these texts frequently contain Latin phrases and passages. Certainly, the use of Latin tag phrases was very common in the culture, and knowledge of some brief snippets of Latin may be assumed among a wider group of individuals than those who had received formal language training. Certainly, in this regard, works of prose fiction are much like the majority of Elizabethan prose composed by and for a humanistically educated audience, but that audience, because of prevailing societal attitudes about the kinds of education boys and girls should receive, was primarily male. What, then, are the implications of the use of Latin within prose fictions directed to female readers? How did these women readers experience fictional texts that assumed facility with a language they were not generally encouraged to learn?

It is difficult to trace just how much Latin girls were typically taught during the last quarter of the sixteenth century. Early in the century, Juan Luis Vives laid out a plan of study for his pupil, the Princess Mary, that included a rigorous Latin education. He had also argued in his *Instruction of a Christian Woman* (1523; trans. Richard Hyrde [1540]) that certain classical authors, including Cicero, should be read by educated women (Watson 137–49, 62). How widely applied his principles were remains unclear. Girls whose education depended heavily on formal schooling outside the home seem most often to have been taught proficiency in domestic skills and how to read English (Spufford 34).[14] A. Monroe Stowe, in his documentary survey of educational practices of the period, *English Grammar Schools in the Reign of Queen Elizabeth,* notes that grammar schools, whose curricula typically included Latin, were usually open only to boys. He cites only two exceptions: in Berkhamsted the statutes state that no limitations were to be placed on students based on "'age, sex, locality or condition of parents'" (126); in Bunbury girls were permitted to attend the local grammar school, but their numbers were limited, and they could not remain in school "above the age of nine nor longer than they may learn to read English" (127). There were, of course, exceptions. Some girls were fortunate enough—like Margaret Roper and the other members of the More family and, later, Rachel Speght— to receive a humanist education; Margaret King asserts that there were approximately sixty such women in Tudor England (208). Nonetheless, the shame Roger Ascham seems to feel Queen Elizabeth's erudition should cause English men suggests that her scholarly attainments were perceived as quite unusual: "It is your shame (I speak to you all, you young Gentlemen of England) that one maid should go beyond you all in excellency of learning, and knowledge of divers tonges"(829). Lisa Jardine has analyzed such responses to humanistically educated women (although in fifteenth-century Italy, not sixteenth-century England), concluding that such women were viewed as rarities. Because humanist education was primarily intended as professional training for men about to enter a public life, Jardine asks, what goal could such an education have for a woman? ("O Decus Italiae Virgo" 817).[15] Culturally, the value of such an education was quite limited. Even Vives, while advocating that the Princess Mary learn Latin and including Cicero among the writers that educated women should read, argues that "as for the knowledge of grammar, logic, histories, the rule of governance of the commonwealth, and the art mathematical, they shall leave it to men. Eloquence is not convenient nor fit for women" (qtd. in Watson 205–6).

An examination of the use of Latin in prose fiction addressed at least partly toward female readers may therefore suggest ways in which some Elizabethan fiction maintained a problematic, anxious relationship with cultural attitudes toward gender, hegemonic educational attitudes, and the humanist agenda. Works as varied as John Lyly's *Euphues: The Anatomy of Wit* (1571), George Gascoigne's *The Adventures of Master F. J.* (1573), and Thomas Lodge's *A Margarite of America* (1594) combine appeals to a female audience with the use of Latin. They simultaneously invite female participation and erect barriers to it, and they prevent the nonhumanistically educated female reader from having full access to the texts' meaning. It is the nature of this conflicting pair of impulses that I wish to explore more fully through the following discussion of one romance that relies heavily on the use of Latin. In this text, Robert Greene's *Ciceronis Amor: Tullies Love,* it seems that control of Latin is given over to female characters in a way that reflects anxiety over the period's dominant ideology of gender relations even at a historical moment when most of Greene's nonelite female readers would have been discouraged from receiving the humanist education they would need in order to fully understand the romance.

Dallying with Terentia

> *Tullie,* notwithstanding his great grauitie *Alternis vicibus* dallied with his *Terentia.*
> —Robert Parry, *Moderatus* (1595)

Ciceronis Amor was one of Greene's most popular romances, issued in nine editions before 1639 (Larson, *Critical Edition,* xlii).[16] In the text's dedication to Lord Strange, Greene claims that the work is an attempt "to pen downe the loves of *Cicero,* which *Plutarch,* and *Cornelius Nepos,* forgot in their writings" (2), but the romance itself seems to draw only names from these authors, and the characters who bear these names often display only slight similarities to their historical counterparts.[17] It describes the courtship of Cicero, here seen primarily as a powerful and persuasive orator of humble origins, and Terentia, a beauty who has committed herself to a life of virginity—Elaine V. Beilin has likened her to Spenser's Belphoebe (117). It also emphasizes the friendship between and rivalry with Lentulus, who in the text is Cicero's chief competitor for Terentia's love and who, as Plutarch reports, was one of Cicero's chief political opponents. The romance describes the process by which Terentia is persuaded to renounce the virgin life and, ultimately, marry Cicero. Along the way the narrative includes Lentulus's attempt to employ Cicero to plead his suit to her, the finding of a suitable mate for Lentulus, and the rehabilitation and marriage of Fabius, a senator's son, to a deserving woman. A pastoral interlude in the "vale of Love" (84) during which the six characters learn of the love between two shepherds, Phillis and Coridon, helps to further the appropriate unions that lead to the text's happy ending.

Greene's romance contains at least twenty-two Latin sentences or phrases of more than two words, but they are not handled consistently. Typically Greene leaves the Latin he employs untranslated; on five particular occasions, however, the romance provides its readers with a clear English paraphrase. Most of the individual examples of Latin phrases remain untranslated—their proverbial nature presumably would make them easily understood by readers. The two instances of more extended untranslated Latin—a three-line quotation from Ennius, which Greene probably derived from a reading of Cicero's *De Officiis,* and a twelve-line poem Archias recites as part of an oration at a banquet—assume a readership well-enough schooled to comfortably translate literary Latin.[18] Both of these Latin passages, moreover, especially that drawn from the *De Officiis* (itself a tract on male virtues and male relationships), emphasize the proper conduct of a public man and are consistent with Renaissance masculinist humanist teaching—the Ennius lines praise a Roman general for his military strategy, and Archias's poem (most likely by Greene himself) speaks in broad terms about the need to reject jealousy. When the sentiments expressed by the Latin, however, challenge the kind of ideological position advocated by Elyot's *The Book Named the Governor* or Ascham's *The Scholemaster,* for instance, or reflect anxiety over gender-based power relations, Greene's use of Latin becomes more complex and more likely to be supplemented with English.

Greene's text reveals a deep ambivalence regarding gender relations as they are established and reinforced by Elizabethan attitudes toward the education of women.

There are three extended instances in which Greene's romance amplifies the Latin text with an English translation. The first occurs during a banquet scene early in the work: "*Lentulus* letting fall his knyfe on his trencher saide aloude, *Non fortuna non Bellum* meaning that neither the highest state of fortune nor the fatall intent of warre could conquere that hart that her beautie hath made subject" (21–22). In this case, the Latin phrase itself is brief, but it prompts a detailed English gloss as Lentulus then narrates an anecdote further contextualizing its meaning. We also receive the translation of a poem Lentulus writes about Terentia and of the letter Cicero writes under Lentulus's name to woo her. The final example of translated Latin in Greene's work is, of course, the title itself.

Greene's text—focusing on a historical figure central to sixteenth-century humanist education and claiming that the work represents the portion of Cicero's life that his Roman biographers accidentally excluded[19]—overtly engages itself on at least one level with an educated, humanist, and (therefore) largely male audience. Greene's desire to reach such a readership is made clear by his reference to himself as "Robert Greene *in artibus magister*" (an allusion to his Oxford and Cambridge education) on the title page of *Ciceronis Amor* and other works, and by his repeated statements about the value of learning.[20] He shows his estimation of the practical value of Latin in his description of the usurer Gorinus, in *Greenes Groatsworth of Witte* (1592), that "Latin hee had some where learned, which though it were but little, yet it was profitable";[21] representations of Greene himself in such works as Henry Chettle's *Kinde-Harts Dreame* (1592) and John Dickenson's *Greene in Conceipt* (1598) as a character who speaks Latin further attest to the cultural perception of him as a figure who values the learning of Latin.[22] This attempt to align the text with a humanist audience is further asserted by Greene's dedicatory epistle to Lord Strange, who is termed a "Maecenas" (3), in a letter heavily laden with classical references. Regardless of these appeals, however, at significant moments within the text—moments that reflect anxiety over heterosexual power relations—*Ciceronis Amor* undermines its appeal to a largely male, humanistically trained audience by seeming to lose confidence in the ability of such readers to use their Latin to read his work.

The first instance of a translated Latin passage occurs at a particularly important textual moment. As we have already observed, at a feast hosted by Terentia's father in honor of Lentulus's military successes against the Parthians, Lentulus, already in love with Terentia, sighs *"Non fortuna non Bellum."* A character who hears his comment wants more than the brief English paraphrase the narrator provides: he seeks an amplification of "this soudaine embleme" (22), which prompts Lentulus to narrate his meeting with a vanquished Parthian lord who—to avoid separation from his wife or dishonor in captivity—had killed his wife and decreed that *"Non fortuna non Bellum"* would separate him from her and so kills himself. This instance provides more than a simple translation—it contextualizes the remark and begins Lentulus's public pursuit of Terentia, but it also helps to link the text's anxiety about leaving Latin untranslated with issues of heterosexual love and gender. What must be explained is a phrase that asserts Lentulus's admission that his heart had been conquered by Terentia. It asserts her power over him. The classification of the Latin phrase as an "embleme" removes it from the category of pure speech—it becomes reified, an artifact distanced from the conversational norm and limited in its ability to convey meaning independently. When Latin, in other words, is linked to undermining the dominance of male control, it requires amplification by English just as the visual images of conventional Renaissance emblems require their accompanying verse.

Later in the text the more striking examples of translated Latin occur: Lentulus's poem on Terentia's beauty and the letter to Terentia that Cicero writes under Lentulus's name. Lentulus's twelve-line poem is reported first in Latin:

Qualis in aurora splendescit lumine Titan,
    Talis in eximio corpore forma fuit:
Lumina seu spectes radiantia, siue capillos,
    Lux Ariadne tua et lux tua Phoebe iacet.
Venustata fuit verbis, spirabat odorem,
    Musica vox, nardus spiritus almus erat:
Rubea labra, genae rubrae, faciesque decora,
    In qua concertant lilius atque rosa.
Luxuriant geminae formoso in pectore mammae,
    Circundant niueae candida colla comae:

Denique talis erat diuina Terentia, quales
   Quondam certantes, Juno, Minerua, Venus. (53–54)

The narrator then translates the poem into English, preceding the translation with the simple phrase, "Thus in English" (54), which seems a highly
disingenuous comment even if we acknowledge that Elizabethan translations tended to be extremely loose. A cursory glance at the poem reveals
that the English text is markedly different from its Latin "equivalent":

Brightsume Apollo in his richest pompe,
   Was not like to the tramels of hir haire:
Hir eyes like Ariadnes sparkling starres,
   Shone from the Ebon Arches of his browes.
Hir face was like the blushing of the east,
   When Titan chargde the mornings Sun to rise:
Hir cheekes rich strewd with roses and with whyte,
   Did stayne the glorie of Anchises loue.
Hir siluer teates did ebbe and flowe delight,
   Hir necke colummes of polisht Ivorie.
Hir breath was perfumes made of violets,
   And all this heauen was but Terentia. (54)

The narrator's brief evaluative comment follows the second version of
the poem: "No sooner had *Lentulus* ended his well written Poem and concluded his cunning with the name of his mistresse" (54), but only one of the
poems, the English version, concludes with Terentia's name—if we are to
understand that Lentulus is in love with Terentia and not with love itself.
To cite two other obvious alterations, Apollo and Anchises (ll.1 and 8 of the
English poem) are nowhere to be found in the Latin text; Phoebe is excised
from the English verse. Of course, there are logical links between the two
different versions. The "Titan" of the Latin's first line, for instance, appears
in line six of the English version, and the addition of Apollo to the opening
of the English serves to amplify the reference to the sun that the Latin contains. In addition, the replacement of the three goddesses of the Latin's
conclusion with Terentia in the English suggests, as Beilin has observed,
that Terentia embodies the qualities of the goddesses erased from the English translation: majesty, intelligence, and beauty (121).

The English poem's emphasis on Terentia at its conclusion may stress her centrality to Lentulus's emotions, but more significant than the implications of the individual semantic and syntactic changes between the poems is the text's silent assumption that the discrepancies between the two poems will go unremarked by its readers. Greene seems to assume either that the differences between the versions of the poem will not be observed because his readers lack humanist training in Latin or that readers educated enough to have read the Latin will not think the differences significant given the culture's perception of the act of translation or that if the differences that seem so glaring to us do register with such readers, then they will keep such information to themselves and not share it with those readers (perhaps especially women readers?) who lack knowledge of Latin. Seen in this way, the poem and its translation may also be viewed as Greene's joke at the expense of the Latin-less.

Shortly after this instance of free translation, Cicero writes a letter of courtship for his friend. The letter, roughly a page and a half in its Latin version, approximately two pages in English, does not present the marked differences we have observed about the poem just discussed.[23] In this instance, Greene's Latin text does seem to have attempted a generally Ciceronian style, and the English translation roughly parallels the Latin epistle. There are none of the radical discrepancies that mark the two versions of Lentulus's poem, although there are of course rearrangements of clauses from the Latin to the English. Minor differences do occur, most notably in the translation of the brief Latin phrase *suavissima Terentia* (57) as "sweete soveraigne of my thoughts, and chief myrrour of our *Romaine* excellencie" (58). Both letters emphasize Terentia's beauty, Lentulus's desire to be her husband, and the honor Terentia would bring to her family by choosing him. In the English version of the letter, however, Lentulus makes an interesting contradiction, building perhaps on his earlier *"Non fortuna non Bellum"*: at one point he asserts that he "hath left his fortunes to followe fancy" (59), suggesting an oppositional relationship between his military career (his fortunes) and his love for Terentia (fancy). Later in the letter, however, he asks her to "measure his fortunes by his fancies" (60). His life as a soldier by the time of this statement has been conflated with his love for her: it is his love for her that defines him. In the Latin, no equivalent of "fancy" is used in either instance. The suggestion here is that Lentulus's primary military identity, especially as it is presented early in the text, is eradicated by his love for

Terentia. Reid Barbour has suggested that the two versions of the letter, like the two versions of the poem, simply demonstrate Greene's interest in "stylistic play" within the romance, an interest that ultimately "subsumes the narrative" (39–40).[24] Such an assessment, while it recognizes the emblematic function of these embedded texts, misses the connections between the Latin and English versions of the documents and the dominant gender concerns of Greene's romance. In the case of the English version of the letter, Lentulus's abandonment of his identity through rejection of his military life is made more explicit, his dependence on Terentia is emphasized, and her identity as a member of the Roman world is made clear.[25] In other words, this letter contains Lentulus's admission of Terentia's power to determine his identity and his "fortunes." Moreover, Lentulus's statement (through Cicero's text) that his identity as a soldier has been negated by Terentia links him to humanist training that, as Mary Thomas Crane observes, in the sixteenth century replaces "aristocratic training in martial skills with a conspicuously nonviolent education in discursive skills" (55).

Although the amount of textual space Greene devotes to providing both versions of the letter is noteworthy, what seems almost more significant is the manner in which the letter is described and contextualized, and the reaction it evokes from the characters to whom it is read. Greene asserts the historical veracity of this letter, saying that

> Terentia kept the copy secrete, so that neither it can bee founde amongst Lentulus loose papers, nor in the familiar epistles of Cicero. If the phrase differ from his other excellent forme of writing, imagine he sought to cover his style, and in his pen rather to play the blunt souldier, then the curious Orator. (56)

The reader, then, is asked to read the Latin letter—and its English translation—as Cicero's own work, but disguised and subtly altered to emulate Lentulus's style. The narrator further asserts the strength of the Latin by apologizing for the translation: "If gentlemen I have not translated *Lentulus* letter verbatim worde for worde, let me in mine owne excuse yeelde these reasons, that neither the familiar phrase of the *Romaines* can brooke our harsh cadence of sentences: nor durst I attempt to wrest Tullies eloquence to my rude and barbarous english" (60). Not only does this statement permit the narrator to emphasize the subtleties of Latin to those gentlemen readers equipped to evaluate the relative rhetorical strengths of Latin and

English, but it also allows him to question the ability of his English to convey complex rhetoric and emotions.[26] This sense of language's limitations will be further emphasized during the final moments of the romance, as Terentia's tears couple with her words during her appearance before the Roman Senate to increase her persuasiveness.

The letter is delivered to Terentia while she is accompanied by Cornelia and Flavia, the two patrician women who will eventually marry Fabius and Lentulus. The response of the women who read the letter deserves particular emphasis. Although the narrator had been concerned about the reaction of the gentlemen readers, it is Flavia, ultimately Lentulus's mate, who remarks almost immediately after hearing the letter that "I durst pawne my credite it was written by young *Tullie* that brave Orator: for I have red some of his Epistles, and tis both his methode and his verie phrase" (63–64), an assessment that Terentia apparently accepts, because it is reflection on this letter that prompts her to fall in love with Cicero. In other words, the power to evoke, control, and understand Latin is given into the hands of the female characters in Greene's romance. It is they who quickly are able to read through the rhetoric to its meaning, not focusing on the Latin as a reified emblem, but rather perceiving the unspoken nuances that the language suggests about its meaning and its author.

The linguistic prowess ascribed to women, as seen in Flavia's perspicacity here, receives a further final confirmation during the text's closing scene in the Roman senate. Although this scene contains no Latin, it does contain two formal speeches to the Roman senators in order to help them determine whom Terentia should marry and how to avoid the impending civil war that her rejection of Lentulus and Fabius has provoked. Cicero delivers a lengthy oration (and Greene calls our attention to it as such by titling it within the text as "Tullies Oration to the Senate"), which asserts Terentia's right to choose to marry him and recounts the struggle of Lentulus and Cicero to honor their friendship to each other while becoming rivals for Terentia's affections and which prompts murmurs of support from the "common people" (122), but the senators themselves are moved only to ask Terentia to defend her choice of husband. Her speech is rhetorically rich. She says in part:

> Before so honourable an audience as these grave Senators and worthy Romayne Citizens womens reasons would seeme no reasons, especially in love which is without reason, therefore I only yeld this reason, I love *Cicero* not able to ratefie my affection with anie strong

reason, because love is not circumscript within reasons limits, but if it please the Senate to pacifie this mutinie, let *Terentia* leave to live, because she cannot leave to love and onely to love *Cicero*. (122)

Her speech smacks of oratorical savvy worthy of Cicero or of humanistically trained readers, although stylistically it seems more to echo the rhetoric of popular Elizabethan romance. Moreover, it is her speech that persuades the Senate and people that she and Cicero should be married, and the text concludes one sentence after her speech, transgressing the bounds of language and becoming emblematic as its meaning is enacted physically, gives way to tears.

Greene's romance, which on the narrative level so overtly invokes the humanist practice of Latin education, reveals a deep distrust of the ways in which that system reifies male speech and relationships and devalues women's intellectual and interpretive skills. That distrust transfers the power to interpret Latin correctly and use language effectively from men to women. Perhaps, in the context of Greene's career, this is not completely startling. Richard Helgerson, basing his comments at least in part on Greene's statements about the content of his first romance, *Mamillia* (1580), calls Greene "the self-proclaimed champion of women"; Helgerson further notes that after Nashe published *The Anatomy of Absurdity*, which satirizes those who praise women and refers to Greene as "the Homer of women," Greene began to repudiate his defense of women, although Helgerson asserts that *Ciceronis Amor* does not "contain any trace of this fugitive misogyny"(94–95).[27] I would go further: Greene's text seems constructed to indicate serious anxiety about the relationship between humanist learning and women and, in fact, it seems to advocate an antimisogynistic position. Greene's use of Latin in this text— from Flavia's ready ability to see that Cicero is the true author of Lentulus's letter to the translation only of Latin that emphasizes the power of female sexuality—suggests the limitations of humanist training and, in particular, of the general exclusion of women from that educational system. It is contact with the female, specifically Terentia, that generates active power, not the humanist training that gave Greene himself such a sense of pride.

Women, it seems, trigger awareness of the limitations of Latin. When confronted by them—their sexuality, the power of their love, the power of their analytical skills—Latin (and humanism along with it) fails. It is Terentia's oration, which reminds us more of the Elizabethan romance than it does of the Ciceronian period, and the tears that accompany it that the Senators find persuasive.[28] It is longing for Terentia that prompts Lentulus's *"Non fortuna non Bellum."* Still, although Latin becomes emblematic and insufficient in the romance, Greene is unwilling to abandon it: the women readers so often appealed to in Elizabethan romances are here given the Latin text but not allowed to rely on it. They evoke it, interpret it, and call forth its limitations; they become central to our understanding of the limitations of a gender ideology that places control of learning in male hands. And this anxious relation to humanist learning may be found in other of Greene's works: *Menaphon* (1589), for instance, which is dedicated "To the right Worshipfull and vertuous Ladie, the Ladie Hales, wife to the late deceased Sir Iames Hales," contains a female character who is able to use untranslated Latin:

Sweete Lamedon, once partner of my royalties, now partaker of my wants, as constant in his extreame distresse, as faithfull in higher fortunes: the Turtle pearketh not on barren trees. Doues delight not in foule cottages, the Lyon frequents no putrified haunts, friends followe not after pouertie, nor hath sinister chance anie drugges from the Phisitians, *Nullus ad amissas ibit amicus opes:* and yet Lamedon the misfortune of Sephestia abridgeth not our olde contracted amitie, thou temperest her exyle with thy banishment, and she sayling to Styx, thou ferriest ouer to Phlegeton: then Lamedon, saying as Andromache sayd to Hector *Tu Dominus, tu vir, tu mihi frater eris.* Thy aged yeres shalbe the calender of my fortunes, and thy gray haires the Paralells of mine actions. If Lamedon perswade Sephestia to content, Portia shall not exceede Sephestia in patience; if he will her to keepe a low sayle, she will vayle al her sheete; if to forget her loues, shee will quench them with labours; if to accuse Venus as a foe, I wil hate Cupide as an enemie: and seeing the Destinies haue driuen thee from a crowne, I will rest satisfied with the Countrey, placing all my delights in honouring thee, & nursing vp my pretie wanton. I will imagine a small cotage to a spacious pallaice, & thinke as great quiet in a russet coate, as in royall habilliments: Sephestia Lamedon will not scorne with Iuno to turne hir self into the shape of Semeles nurse, but vnknowne rest carelesse of my fortunes: the hope of times returne shal be the ende of my thoughts, the smiles of my sonne shall bee the nourishment of my hart, and the course of his youth shall be the comfort of my yeres; euerie laughter that leapes from his lookes, shall be the holiday of my conceiptes, and euerie teare, shal furnish out my greeues, and his fathers funerals. I haue heard them say Lamedon, that the lowest shrubbes feele the least tempests, that in the valleis of Affrica is heard no thunder, that in countrey roomes is greatest rest, and in little wealth the least disquiet: dignitie treadeth vpon glasse, and honour is like to the hearbe Synara, that when it bloometh most gorgeous, then it blasteth: *Aulica vita splendida miseria,* Courts haue golden dreames, but cotages sweet slumbres: then Lamedon will I disguise my self, with my cloathes I will change my thoughts; for being poorelie attired I will be meanelie minded, and measure my actions by my present estate, not by former fortunes. (28–29)

Her Latin is as casually inserted into her discourse as into any humanist text, though the female characters in this work are not given to this kind of use of Latin generally. Similarly, in Greene's *Gwydonius: The Carde of Fancy* (1584), a work that contains both translated and untranslated Latin, the title character uses untranslated Latin during a debate with Castania, the woman whom he loves and whom he wants to be able to understand his language:

And shall then Madame (quoth he) my merite be repayed with no meede, shall my good will be requited with no gain? shal I haue in lieu of my loue no liking? will you so swarne from Iustice, as not to giue euerye one according to his desert? at the least recompence: not desire with despight, and heartie loue with loathing hate, for as the Poet sayeth. *Quis emni succenset amanti.*

And her response reveals that she has understood his meaning:

Well Gwydonius, as I will not be thy priuie friend, so I will not be thine open foe, and as I cannot be so curteous as to requight thee for thy paines, so I wil not bee so cruell as to despight thee for thy presumption, and whereas thou crauest gaines for thy good will, I am content to remaine thy vnwilling debter. (77–78)

In Greene's texts, in other words, use of humanist Latin is qualified to include women, to provide them with access to the knowledge of the world that it contains. It is not used, as it had been by Lyly or Grange, to exclude women from such knowledge. Such misuse of Latin is further emphasized by Thomas Nashe who, in his preface to *Menaphon,* had praised those serious humanists, such as Erasmus and Melancthon, who had translated Greek works into Latin and in so doing had "reedified the ruines of our decayed Libraries, and merueilouslie inriched the Latine tongue with the expence of their toyle" (11); however, such erudition has not been transposed to the majority of English writers. Among writers in his own country, he condemns those who imitate the Continental humanists, remarking that "euerie priuate Scholler, . . . beganne to vaunt their smattering of Latine, in English Impressions" (11): Nashe's *The Unfortunate Traveller* is itself full of untranslated Latin as it addresses its ostensibly courtly audience.

I would suggest that Greene's *Ciceronis Amor* takes great pride in the ability to drop untranslated Latin into the work and to see the work less as romance than as a historical document filling in the gaps in the knowledge of his humanistically trained audience about Cicero's biography. Greene would, it seems, have been pleased to have such studious readers as Lady Jane Grey. But Greene simultaneously wants "delight" as well—he wants his male and female readers both to read "a merie tale," as Ascham put it, as well as a biography of a figure central to humanist education. Greene's romance seems to suggest that providing women with access to such learning would unleash women's interpretive powers and demonstrate the limitations of prevailing educational practices. Unlike his humanist predecessors, like Vives, Greene in this text seems to see eloquence as "convenient" and "fit" for women, even if patriarchal structures are threatened as a result. It was, perhaps, a safe position to advocate textually because it was unthinkable pragmatically.

The complex ambivalence toward humanism, gender relations, and romance readership delineated in the previous discussion is also revealed in the final example of translated Latin within Greene's romance: its title. *Ciceronis Amor: Tullies Love* may be paraphrased in English in two ways: "The Progress of the Emotion of Love through the Heart of Cicero" or simply as "Terentia." The title, in other words, both foregrounds Cicero's struggle and names its female protagonist. The two are not separated. And the ambiguity of the phrase is repeated by its English translation. Once again the text emphasizes the limitations of Latin and humanist education and the centrality of women to those limitations. The way in which Latin is used here, in other words, parallels the way in which fictional locations are used in *Pandosto* or *The Patterne of Painefull Adventures*: it encourages readers to see the text as a "glasse" that will provide factual information about a foreign and distant culture. What it delivers, however, under this guise, is the undermining of cultural values and the propagation of fiction.

Conclusion

THE GEOGRAPHY OF FISHWIVES, OR WHO'S SHE WHEN SHE'S AT HOME?

This study has explored the ways in which fictional representation of cultural difference in Elizabethan prose fiction is tightly bound up with representations of gender and with the period's ethnographic and travel discourse. The fictions of the period used the language and techniques of the travel report to create attitudes about cultural difference, and the impact of that alienating effect often becomes most clearly manifest in the female characters of the texts. As such, much early modern prose fiction may be seen as helping to lay the groundwork for the later language of the British Empire and the culture's continuing misogyny. This argument, however, leaves unexplored the links between the representations of gender and geography when the locations depicted are not foreign but English. What happens when the "glasse" is turned back on England itself, when it examines the "self" instead of the "other"?

Although these questions merit more detailed analysis than may be provided here, I would like to consider one text that brings home the issues of gender and geography to show that the ideological impulses operating in the representation of cultural difference are equally present when England is the geographic space described.

Westward for Smelts, a 1620 collection of novellas presented within a Chaucerian frame tale, provides a useful text for exploring the links between gender and geography in the fictional representations of England because it diverges from the kinds of novella collections discussed in chapter 2 in two significant respects: it creates six English fishwives who function as the work's storytellers, and it sets its tales in England, not in the European and Eastern locations typically found in Boccaccio's early modern English successors. These tales, which the text describes as "wholesome though homely," present various kinds of marital infidelity, jealousy, and thwarted sexual desire through the voice of lower-class female narrators, a combination that creates an argument for the kind of utopian vision possible in early modern culture—for the kind of geographic "home" the text's fishwives can create.

Westward for Smelts was allegedly written by "Kind Kit of Kingston," who also serves as the ferryman-narrator transporting six fishwives home after they have sold their wares to a fish-hungry London population during Lent. Kit proposes to sing his passengers a song to keep them awake on their trip; the women promise to each tell a tale in payment for it. Kit's song is a forty-line poem about a young man's love for a beautiful woman who is both immodestly forthcoming and yet perceived as aloof. She partially disrobes, teasing the man; yet he feels that "Had I made a tryall, / Her most sad deniall, / My obseruant heart oh[!] it would breake" (9), so he determines to content himself with the "private pleasures" she showed him. Kit asks the fishwives for their response to his song:

> Hauing thus ended, I asked them how they liked my Song? They said little to it. At last, Well, quoth a venerable Matron (or rather a Matron of Uenery) that sate on a Cushion at the vpper end of the Boat, let vs now performe our promises to him in telling euery one her Tale. (9)

Their complete nonresponse to his question indicates a rejection of Kit's tale and of the worldview it suggests. The wives' reaction to the fourth tale, told by the Fishwife of Twitnam, makes this clear. The tale involves the seventh-century St. Oswald of Northumbria and his Queen, Beblam, who, after the birth of a son, decide to live celibate, holy lives. A hermit doubts that it is possible to have a wife and yet live a life of holiness, so the King sends him to Beblam with instructions that she "should use him in all respects as shee would use himselfe" (48). As a result, the hermit receives only bread and water to eat instead of a feast, and he is thrown into a well twice because he believes that an invitation into the Queen's bed is an invitation to intercourse. He concludes that Oswald and Beblam do live holy lives.

The fishwives agree that Beblam is virtuous but that she "was not to be any president for them, seeing shee was a queene, and they were but fishwives." One further argues that their husbands would never tolerate such chastity: "Therefore for my part, I will never go about it" (51), she says. The women, in other words, are highly sensitive to their economic and social position. The world that Beblam inhabited is not theirs, despite the didactic intentions of the storyteller to describe a woman "whose life may bee a mirrour for all women" (47).

The stories the women tell describe their world, and it is one of bleak confinement. These stories occupy domestic spaces in which women are attacked, as is Beblam by the hermit, and where control is taken from them. And when women in these tales do travel from their homes their attempts at independence generally lead to attack or imprisonment as well. These women suffer a range of kinds of domestic abuse: one is tied to a post by her front door, several have their bedrooms invaded by would-be rapists, another is routinely locked into her house at night and must steal the key from her husband to gain some liberty, and in the final tale a woman is literally imprisoned for her treatment of her suitor. It is a depressing list. In this final story, the woman's rationale for the harsh behavior that results in her imprisonment makes explicit the rules governing the confinement of women in the other tales. She explains to her suitor that "such little libertie hath our sexe, and men such corrupt judgements, that . . . it behooveth us to bee carefull over ourselves, and not through our kindnesses to give inconstant and dissembling men occasion to speake ill" (59). Her harshness toward him, in other words, results from her sense of perpetual cultural imprisonment.

What makes the sense of female confinement more stunning in these tales is their female narrators and their geographic placement within England. The text's use of King Oswald and his queen, for instance, to inhabit a tale of marital chastity, provides one example. The geography of another story, an analogue for the wager plot in *Cymbeline,* provides another. Although there are many versions of this narrative, it is Boccaccio's version in the *Decameron* (2.9) that is generally best known.[1] Boccaccio's tale involves Italian merchants who meet in a Parisian inn. The abused wife disguises herself as a sailor who serves first a Catalonian gentleman and then becomes a trusted member of the Sultan of Alexandria's forces. In that capacity she is sent to an international assembly of merchants at Acre, where she effects her vindication and the punishment of her abuser.

The geographic framing of the tale undergoes extensive revision and contraction in *Westward for Smelts,* in which the narrative sets the home of the central couple in "Waltam" during "the troublesome reigne of King Henry the sixt" (20). The wager between the husband and the unnamed villain is contracted at a London inn, and the place of the innocent woman's "execution" is identified as "Enfield." In his sorrow over his wife's presumed infidelity, the husband undertakes to serve "King Henry, who a little before was inlarged by the Earle of Warwicke, and placed in the throne againe" (28). The wife, in her male disguise, serves as a page to "King Edward (being come out of France, and lying thereabouts [at York] with the small forces he had)" (31) until, after the Battle of Barnet, Henry's forces are defeated, both her husband and her accuser are captured, and the latter's identity is discovered by her. The scene then shifts to London, where she has the villain treated for his battle wounds and then prompts King Edward to "doe her justice on a villain that had been the cause of all the misery she had suffered" (33).[2] Place has clearly become more narrowly defined—both in geographic and historical terms: the Battle of Barnet occurred in 1471 between Edward IV and Henry VI; Enfield is selected as the spot for her execution because it is approximately halfway between London and Waltham.

A final geographic reference finds its way into the fishwives' discussion of the tale following its conclusion. The wife of Brainford calls the virtuous woman of the narrative "a garment out of fashion [who] . . . would shew as vild as a paire of Yorkeshire sleeves in a goldsmithes shop" (36). The story, in other words, is transferred entirely into the confines of England, centered around one of the most tumultuous times in England's history, and reduced to the occasion for a mention of provincial English fashions. Interestingly this morsel of cultural information has a parallel in Boccaccio's version of the tale. At the end of that text, Boccaccio reports of the villain:

> The very same day that he was impaled on a stake, anointed with honey, and fixed in the place appointed to his mean torment, he not only died but likewise was devoured to the bare bones by flies, wasps, and hornets, whereof the country notoriously aboundeth. (200)[3]

The novella's "glasse" must be focused on a geographically didactic detail: we don't learn about the nature of Yorkshire fashions, but we do learn that in the world governed by Boccaccio's Sultan, the bugs are ferociously different from those of Christian Europe. In both texts, while we support the just resolutions of the tales, our comfortable identification with those resolutions is geographically distanced by geographic information that emphasizes our alienation from those cultures.

The geographic contraction of the tale in *Smelts* is paired with the fairly unusual use of an entirely nonaristocratic set of female narrators and implied audience. The effect of this contraction, of this insularity, is the creation of an idealized working-class female state. Moreover, this floating female utopia of fishwives is concerned with the lives of women in England. As the *Cymbeline* analogue suggests, the resolution of the problems that the tales pose may also be found within England. These women express a belief in the self-sufficiency of English tales, English history, and English customs to create their culture. Moreover, the isolation of these women in a boat on the Thames (and at one point they actively choose to continue floating past their destinations so that they might continue to tell their tales) hints at the possible existence of such a utopian vision only in the watery, unanchored world of the Thames.

The status of fishwives in early modern England reinforces the lack of fixed cultural identity or cultural memory visible in *Smelts*. As "foreigners"[4] coming into London to sell their fish, fishwives were seen as a disruptive force in need of regulation. Through the 1580s, laws required fishwives to "pass along the streets and lanes of the city"[5] selling their wares. This attempt to reduce competition between these women and the established London markets separates them from the formal guild-based market system, distancing them from identification with London and the nascent nationalism emerging from its culture in the late sixteenth and early seventeenth centuries. The separation of fish sellers, both male and female, from identification with notions of nationhood and national memory may be further deduced from John Stow's statement that he included in his *Survey* a brief history of the fishmongers' guild, because they are "men ignorant of their antiquities."[6] The anchorless fishwives of *Smelts* create a political identity for themselves through a fantastic, utopian narrative structure and content that rely on their own notion of "Englishness." The fishwives are excluded from the period's nationalist identity projects by their gender, their foreign status, and their profession. In this text, fiction creates memory, communal identity, and history for those to whom conventional historical narratives do not apply. Despite the ways in which they are alienated from English national identity, the geographic Englishness of both the tellers and their tales constructs a geographic identity for women that gives them agency, narrative authority, and a clearly constructed lived-in space to inhabit. The geographic location of this space, in a boat on the Thames, suggests the continued anxiety English fiction will contain about who may inhabit geographical spaces and suggests that it will alienate many more than it will include.

Notes

Introduction

1. Paul Salzman, *English Prose Fiction, 1558–1700: A Critical History* (Oxford, U.K.: Oxford Univ. Press, 1985), describes Robarts as a writer of popular chivalric romances who gradually became "more of a conveyer of an ideology than a disinterested entertainer" (99). Following Louis B. Wright's lead, he describes Robarts as an increasingly didactic writer determined to spread his own nationalistic views. See also Louis B. Wright, "Henry Robarts: Patriotic Propagandist and Novelist," *Studies in Philology* 29 (1932): 176–99.

2. On the relationship between gender and the experience of reading early modern fiction, see Caroline Lucas, *Writing for Women: The Example of Woman as Reader in Elizabethan Romance* (Philadelphia, Pa.: Open Univ. Press, 1989), and, more recently, Helen Hackett, *Women and Romance Fiction in the English Renaissance* (Cambridge, U.K.: Cambridge Univ. Press, 2000).

3. Michel de Certeau, *The Practice of Everyday Life,* trans. Steven F. Rendall (Berkeley: Univ. of California Press, 1984), 115–30.

1. The Fiction of Ethnography/The Ethnography of Fiction

1. Qtd. in Nick De Somogyi, "Marlowe's Maps of War," in *Christopher Marlowe and English Renaissance Culture,* ed. Daryll Grantley and Peter Roberts (Aldershot, U.K.: Scolar, 1996), 107.

2. Investigations into the nature of the early modern perception of the English nation are greatly indebted to Homi Bhabha's analysis of the ways in which cultural identity is formed and negotiated. In addition to Bhabha's *The Location of Culture* (New York: Routledge, 1994), see also Amy Boesky, *Founding Fictions: Utopias in Early Modern England* (Athens: Univ. of Georgia Press, 1996).

3. See John Gillies, *Shakespeare and the Geography of Difference* (Cambridge, U.K.: Cambridge Univ. Press, 1994), 34–36. These traditional accounts, especially of the non-European world, were based on what O. R. Dathorne calls four kinds of "proto-texts" that were key in creating European views of Asia and Africa: Pliny, Alexandrian romances, the Letter of Prester John, and early texts on the wonders of the East. *Imagining the World: Mythical Belief versus Reality in Global Encounters* (Westport, Conn.: Bergin and Garvey, 1994), 41.

4. My use of this phrase is intended to echo both William Nelson, *Fact or Fiction: The Dilemma of the Renaissance Storyteller* (Cambridge, Mass.: Harvard Univ. Press, 1973), and Lennard J. Davis, *Factual Fictions: The Origins of the English Novel* (New York: Columbia Univ. Press, 1983). Both texts have long influenced my understanding of early modern fiction.

5. Hodgen cites, between 1536 and 1611, twenty-three editions: "9 in Latin, 5 in Italian, 4 in French, 3 or 4 in English, and 1 in Spanish" (132–33). Anthony Grafton calls Boemus "a widely read though not a deeply reflective scholar." *New Worlds, Ancient Texts: The Power of Tradition and the Shock of Discovery* (Cambridge, Mass.: Belknap, 1992), 99.

6. Donald F. Lach and Theodore Nicholas Foss use the phrase to describe what was added during this period to medieval representations of Asia in "Images of Asia and Asians in European Fiction, 1500–1800," in *Asia in Western Fiction*, ed. Robin W. Winks and James R. Rush (Honolulu: Univ. of Hawaii Press, 1990), 18.

7. Qtd. in De Somogyi, "Marlowe's Maps of War," 96.

8. Dedication. Qtd. in Eugene R. Kintgen, "Reconstructing the Interpretive Conventions of Elizabethan Readers," in *Language, Text and Context: Essays in Stylistics*, ed. Michael Toolan (London: Routledge, 1992), 95.

9. For a useful discussion of the connections between early modern travel literature and captivity narratives, see Joe Snader, *Caught between Worlds: British Captivity Narratives in Fact and Fiction* (Lexington: Univ. Press of Kentucky, 2000), 13–61. Another useful overview of the period's English travel literature is provided in Casey Blanton, *Travel Writing: The Self and the World* (New York: Twayne, 1997), 1–29.

10. Edward Webbe's 1590 *The Rare and Most VVonderful Things which Edw. Vvebbe an Englishman Borne, Hath Seene and Passed in His Troublesome Trauailes*, which describes his travels into Asia Minor, Africa, and the Middle East, as well as his captivity by the Turks, also includes a woodcut of a unicorn that Webbe claims to have seen. Snader, *Caught between Worlds*, 32–33, 55.

11. Full title: "*The New Found Worlde, or Antarctike, wherein is contained wo[n]derful and strange things, as well of humaine creatures, as beastes, Fishes, Foules, and Serpents, trees, Plents, Mines of Golde and Siluer: garnished with many learned authorities, trauailed and written in the French tong, by that excellent learned man, master Andrewe Thevet. And now newly translated into Englishe, wherein is reformed the errours of the auncient Cosmographers.*" Quotations are from the edition published in the series the English Experience 417 (New York: Da Capo, 1971). Julia Kristeva comments briefly on Thevet's text in *Strangers to Ourselves*, citing it as one of the most exceptional and popular geographical publications produced during the sixteenth century (123). In

addition, Pamela Neville-Singleton comments that Richard Hakluyt found Thevet's work quite useful as a source. See "'A Very Good Trumpet': Richard Hakluyt and the Politics of Overseas Expansion," in *Texts and Cultural Change in Early Modern England*, ed. Cedric C. Brown and Arthur Marotti (New York: St. Martin's, 1997), 70.

12. Frank Lestringant, *Cannibals: The Discovery and Representation of the Cannibal from Columbus to Jules Verne*, trans. Rosemary Morris (Berkeley: Univ. of California Press, 1997), 46. On Thevet, see esp. 44–49.

13. Jean de Léry, *History of a Voyage to the Land of Brazil* (1578), qtd. in Stephen Greenblatt, *Marvelous Possessions: The Wonder of the New World* (Chicago: Univ. of Chicago Press, 1991), 22.

14. On the nature of the dialogue form in sixteenth-century England, see K. J. Wilson, *Incomplete Fictions: The Formation of English Renaissance Dialogue* (Washington, D.C.: Catholic Univ. Press, 1985).

15. For more on the nature and practice of chorography in the period, see Richard Helgerson, "Writing Empire and Nation," in *The Cambridge Companion to English Literature, 1500–1600*, ed. Arthur F. Kinney (Cambridge, U.K.: Cambridge Univ. Press, 2000), 324–27, and E. G. R. Taylor, *Late Tudor and Early Stuart Geography, 1583–1650* (London: Methuen, 1934), 39–52.

16. Gillies observes, "Like some armchair Tamburlaine, Spoudaeus reduces the world to a map in order to control it," in *Shakespeare and the Geography of Difference*, 92.

17. See Raymond Waddington, "Rewriting the World, Rewriting the Body," in *The Cambridge Companion to English Literature, 1500–1600*, 302.

18. Margaret Cavendish, "The Description of a New World Called the Blazing World," in *An Anthology of Seventeenth-Century Fiction*, ed. Paul Salzman (Oxford: Oxford Univ. Press, 1991), 269.

19. Nicholas de Nicholay, *The Nauigations, Peregrinations, and Voyages, made into Turkie* (London, 1585), English Experience 48 (New York: Da Capo, 1968), 34. All future references to this work will be by page number.

20. For example, janissaries, "Azamoglans" (71), archers, military captains, lackies (82), wrestlers, drunkards, cooks, physicians, Greek peasants, members of various Islamic sects, emirs, and water carriers.

21. Margaret Hodgen, *Early Anthropology in the Sixteenth and Seventeenth Centuries* (Philadelphia: Univ. of Pennsylvania Press, 1964).

22. Ibid., 22.

23. Ibid., 32–33. She is quoting from *The Works of Rabelais*, trans. Sir Thomas Urquart and Peter Anthony Motteaux (London: Bullen, 1904), 3:341–48.

24. George Whetstone, *The English Myrror* (London, 1586), English Experience 632 (New York: Da Capo, 1973).

25. Arthur F. Kinney, "Situational Poetics," *Prose Studies* 11, no. 2 (Sept. 1988): 12. The rhetorical shape and structure of the prose that these texts use, and their reception and consumption within early modern culture, make the ethnographic dimension of the period's prose fiction different from that of the dramatic texts that Gillies discusses.

26. Sir Walter Raleigh, *Sir Walter Raleigh: Selected Writings*, ed. Gerald Hammond (Manchester, U.K.: Carcanet, 1984), 127.

27. From the nonpaginated preface "To the Prince." Complete title: *A Relation of a Iourney begun An: Dom: 1610. Fovre Bookes Containing a description of the Turkish Empire, of Aegypt, of the Holy Land, of the Remote parts of Italy, and Ilands. adioyning. 1615.* Published in the English Experience 554 (New York: Da Capo, 1973). This is the second edition of Sandys's work. For additional discussion of Sandys, see the relevant portions of Ivo Kamps and Jyotsna Singh, eds., *Travel Knowledge: European "Discoveries" in the Early Modern Period* (New York: Palgrave, 2001).

28. Robert Coverte, *A True and Almost Incredible Report of an Englishman* (London, 1612), English Experience 302 (New York: Da Capo, 1971).

29. Neville-Singleton, "'A Very Good Trumpet,'" 68. See also Greenblatt, *Marvelous Possessions,* 30–33 for additional discussion of Hakluyt.

30. Quotations from Hakluyt are from Richard Hakluyt, *Voyages and Discoveries: The Principal Navigations, Voyages, Traffiques and Discoveries of the English Nation,* ed. Jack Beeching (New York: Penguin, 1972). On Hakluyt's representations of cultural difference see, among others, Emily Bartels, "Making More of the Moor: Aaron, Othello, and Renaissance Refashionings of Race," *Shakespeare Quarterly* 41, no. 4 (Winter 1990): 433–54.

31. William Lithgow, *A Discourse of a Peregrination in Europe, Asia and Affricke* (London, 1614), English Experience 399 (New York: Da Capo, 1971). On Catholicism, see his discussion of Loretta, sig. C–C3. See also sig. C3ᵛ: "I commend the deuotion of *Venice & Genua,* beyond all the other cities of *Italy;* for the *Venetians* haue banished the *iesuites* out of their Territories and Ilands: And the *Genueses* haue abandoned the society of *Iewes* & exposed them from their iurisdiction. The *Iews* and the *Iesuits* are brethren in blasphemies; for the *Iewes* are naturally subtill, hatefull, auaritious, & aboue all the greatest calumniators of *Christs* name: And the ambitious *Iesuites,* are flatteres, blody-gospellers, treasonable tale-tellers, and the onely railers vpon the sincere life of good *Christians.* Wherefore I end with this verdict, the *Iew* and the *Iesuite* is a pultrone and a parasite" (sig.C3ᵛ). For additional discussion of Lithgow, see Kenneth Parker, ed., *Early Modern Tales of Orient: A Critical Anthology* (New York: Routledge, 1999), 149–74, and Kamps and Singh, *Travel Knowledge,* 28–52.

32. Gillies explains the differences between Hakluyt and Purchas through their treatment of *Mandeville's Travels.* Hakluyt had excluded this medieval text from his collection because of its fictionality. Purchas reinstated it as the second edition of *Principal Navigations,* demonstrating the text's continued appeal during the period among "less serious geographers" (Gillies 197). See also Greenblatt, *Marvelous Possessions,* 26–51, for additional discussion of *Mandeville's Travels.*

33. See Jeffrey Knapp, *An Empire Nowhere: England, America, and Literature from Utopia to The Tempest* (Berkeley: Univ. of California Press, 1992), 64–65.

34. Helgerson, "Writing," 325.

35. See Ann Hoffman, *Lives of the Tudor Age* (New York: Barnes and Noble, 1977), 251.

36. Quotation of the *Chronicles* are from Henry Ellis's 1807 edition (repr., New York: AMS, 1965) by volume and page number.

37. On English representations of Ireland, see Ann Rosalind Jones and Peter

Stallybrass, "Dismantling Irena: The Sexualizing of Ireland in Early Modern England," in *Nationalisms and Sexualities,* ed. Andrew Parker, Mary Russo, Doris Sommer, and Patricia Yaeger (New York: Routledge, 1992), 157–71.

38. Helgerson, "Writing," 315.

39. Boesky's discussion of early modern utopian fictions makes a related point: she writes that the utopia "is neither a heuristic model nor a historical mirror but a representation of the tensions and ambiguities surrounding the very ideas of nationalism and reform" (9).

40. See also Laurel Richardson and Ernest Lockridge, "Fiction and Ethnography: A Conversation. (Part 2)," *Qualitative Inquiry* 4, no. 3 (Sept. 1998): 328–37, on the continuing intersections between ethnographic reports and fictional prose and the role of didacticism in both.

41. Jonathan Haynes, *The Humanist as Traveler: George Sandys' Relation of a Journey begun An. Dom. 1610* (Rutherford, N.J.: Fairleigh Dickinson Univ. Press, 1986), 86. Plutarch's *Isis and Osiris* is included in his *Moralia.*

2. The Gendered and Geographic "Glasses" of the English Novella

1. Timothy Hampton, *Writing from History: The Rhetoric of Exemplarity in Renaissance Literature* (Ithaca, N.Y.: Cornell Univ. Press, 1990), 30.

2. Ibid.

3. R. W. Maslen, *Elizabethan Fictions: Espionage, Counter-Espionage and the Duplicity of Fiction in Early Elizabethan Prose Narratives* (Oxford, U.K.: Clarendon, 1997), 82. Helen Hackett also analyzes several of the novella collections discussed in this chapter, although she groups them with George Gascoigne's *The Adventures of Master F. J.,* a very different text. Her work will be discussed more fully in chapter 4.

4. William Painter, *The Palace of Pleasure,* 4 vols. (London: Cresset, 1929). All quotations to Painter's text will be to this edition by volume and page. Maslen (88) also discusses the didactic focus of Painter's dedication.

5. Salzman, *English Prose Fiction,* 9. On the didactic dimension of Painter's text and the link between its didacticism and Painter's female readers, especially of the 1567 volume, see Hackett, *Women and Romance Fiction in the English Renaissance,* 35–38. Hackett also discusses the appeals to female readers of Fenton's and Pettie's novella collections.

6. Walter Davis asserts that the early novella usually "maintained an air of factuality whose main attributes were realistic detail and a remorseless detachment from ideals," and he further observes that the novella "usually presents love from the fabliau's point of view, and it presents tragedy in a world unrelieved by divine grace." *Idea and Act in Elizabethan Fiction* (Princeton, N.J.: Princeton Univ. Press, 1969), 155.

7. Geoffrey Fenton, *Certain Tragical Discourses of Bandello,* 2 vols., intro. Robert Langton Douglas (1898; repr., New York: AMS, 1967).

8. Lorna Hutson, *The Usurer's Daughter: Male Friendship and Fictions of Women in Sixteenth-Century England* (New York: Routledge, 1994), 107.

9. On this point, see Ullrich Langer's "The Renaissance Novella as Justice," *Renaissance Quarterly* 52, no. 2 (Summer 1999): 319, which draws on Timothy Hampton's *Writing from History*. Langer calls many of the Continental novellas "civilizing," and argues that "narratives can convey a moral understanding without featuring exemplary behavior, precisely because justice as the underlying logic of the plot can be quite indifferent to the actual merit of any one character" (319).

10. See Jane Collins, "Publishing Private Pleasures: The Gentlewoman Reader of Barnaby Riche and George Pettie," *Explorations in Renaissance Culture* 22, no. 2 (Winter 2003): 185–210, and Juliet Fleming's "The Ladies' Man and the Age of Elizabeth," in *Sexuality and Gender in Early Modern Europe: Institutions, Texts, Images,* ed. James Grantham Turner (Cambridge: Cambridge Univ. Press, 1993), 158–81, as well as Caroline Lucas and Lorna Hutson more generally on the nature of these addresses.

11. Hutson, *The Usurer's Daughter,* 97.

12. There is not room here to raise the significant discursive links between geography and same-sex as well as heterosexual desire; however, Winfried Schleiner, raising briefly one dimension of the complexities of homosexual desire in the period, notes that "Renaissance accounts of 'unnatural acts' ascribe same-sex love to the religious and cultural other, the Turk." "Cross-Dressing, Gender Errors, and Sexual Taboos in Renaissance Literature," in *Gender Reversals and Gender Cultures,* ed. Sabrina Ramet (New York: Routledge, 1996), 98.

13. Bhabha, *The Location of Culture,* 145.

14. 3.62: "From Bandello to the Very Kind Gentleman Domenico Cavazza," in *Italian Renaissance Tales,* trans. Janet Levarie Smarr (Rochester, Mich.: Solaris, 1983), 229–30.

15. This impulse might also be linked to the utopian discursive impulse Boesky ably describes in early modern culture. The idealized representation for culture, as she explains, "depended on inaccessibility" (177). The geographic anxiety of the novella manifests itself by constructing inaccessible locations while simultaneously gesturing toward their accessibility through geographic discourse.

16. Maslen, *Elizabethan Fictions,* 86.

17. Ibid., 90.

18. Note the faithfulness with which Painter translates Marguerite's version of the passage:

[Amadour's] face was contorted with a terrifying violence, as if there was some raging inferno belching fire in his heart and behind his eyes. One powerful fist roughly seized hold of her two weak and delicate hands. Her feet were held in a vice-like grip. There was nothing she could do to save herself. She could neither fight back, nor could she fight free.

Marguerite de Navarre, *The Heptameron,* trans. and ed. P. A. Chilton (New York: Viking Penguin, 1984). All further references to de Navarre's text will be to this edition by page number.

19. Writing of Marguerite's version of the tale, Timothy Hampton similarly asserts that the "question of borders and territories is central to this tale." *Literature and Nation in the Sixteenth Century: Inventing Renaissance France* (Ithaca, N.Y.: Cornell Univ. Press, 2001), 116.

20. Marcel Tetel, *Marguerite de Navarre's Heptameron: Themes, Language, and Structure* (Durham, N.C.: Duke Univ. Press, 1973), 28. Tetel also calls attention to the use of the verb *guerroyer* in tale 10 to describe the verbal exchanges between Amadour and Florinda, further emphasizing the importance of military imagery within the text (29).

21. Here Painter seems to mistranslate Marguerite in the *Heptameron*: "to hide my anger just as . . . I've hidden my joy" (134). In Painter: "to dissemble my anger and contentation." In the *Heptameron* he is not doing both simultaneously. The shift seems part of a plan to ennoble Amadour.

22. Patricia Francis Cholakian, *Rape and Writing in the* Heptameron *of Marguerite de Navarre* (Carbondale: Southern Illinois Univ. Press, 1991), 91.

23. Langer also briefly alludes to the role of place in Navarre's novellas and the early modern novella as a whole, suggesting that references to rulers and the places they govern, which typically occur at the beginning of a narrative, function to establish a framework in which justice will be enacted, thereby permitting satisfying narrative closure (327). For more on the ransoming of European captives in the East and the nature of Mediterranean pirates, see Richard Wilson, "Voyage to Tunis: New History and the Old World of *The Tempest*," *ELH* 64, no. 2 (Summer 1997): 333–57.

24. George Pettie, *A Petite Palace of Pettie His Pleasure*, ed. Herbert Hartman (London: Oxford Univ. Press, 1938), 235–36.

25. René Pruvost, *Matteo Bandello and Elizabethan Fiction* (Paris: Librairie Ancienne Honoré Champion, 1937), 180. Margaret Schlauch finds Fenton guilty, in his eleventh tale, of "Elizabethan stylistic padding at its worst." "English Short Fiction in the Fifteenth and Sixteenth Centuries," *Studies in Short Fiction* 3 (1966): 423.

26. Pruvost, *Matteo Bandello*, 190.

27. Maslen, *Elizabethan Fictions*, 97.

28. Robert Langton Douglas, ed., *Certain Tragical Discourses of Bandello Translated into English by Gefraie Fenton, anno 1567*, 2 vols. (1898; repr., New York: AMS, 1967), 1:163.

29. Pruvost writes of this tale that in Bandello's version it is four pages long; in Fenton's it is forty-five pages long. Fenton "as usual plays sundry rhetorical variations round the text of Belleforest without altering its substance. Everywhere the situations indicated in a few lines by Bandello are developed at great length; everywhere the heroes launch into long speeches; everywhere an attempt is made at analysing their feelings. Particularly noticeable in this respect is the expression of Luchyn's despair when he finds that Janiquetta will not grant him his suit. Here again Belleforest makes him pour his sorrow out in verse. Fenton omits his poetry, but for the rest he consistently follows the lead of his model." Pruvost, *Matteo Bandello*, 158.

Caroline Lucas observes that "Fenton's prose was more rhetorically elaborate than Painter's" and that George Pettie's style is more elaborate than Painter's (42).

This seems a conventional and fair thing to say. Pettie's elaborations become more euphuistic. On the implications of euphuism, see Joan Pong Linton, "The Humanist in the Market: Gendering Exchange and Authorship in Lyly's *Euphues* Romances," in *Framing Elizabethan Fictions,* ed. Constance C. Relihan (Kent, Ohio: Kent State Univ. Press, 1996), 73–97. Euphuism itself serves a didactic aim.

30. Thomas F. Crane in 1920 called it "the most elaborate original production of [its] kind in English literature." *Italian Social Customs of the Sixteenth Century and Their Influence on the Literature of Europe* (New Haven, Conn.: Yale Univ. Press, 1920), 520.

31. On the intricacies of the structure of Marguerite de Navarre's *Heptameron,* see Josephine Donovan's *Women and the Rise of the Novel, 1405–1726* (New York: St. Martin's, 1999), in which she links the early modern framed novella collections, including Navarre's, with the dialogic structure of the novel.

32. Diana Shklanka, ed., *A Critical Edition of George Whetstone's 1583* An Heptameron of Civill Discourses (New York: Garland, 1987), 331. Langer, in his treatment of Navarre's *Heptameron,* discusses novella openings such as this one in the context of their emphasis on the identification of the prevailing ruler who will ultimately "encourag[e] a just resolution of a conflict" (327). He does not specifically discuss Whetstone's text, and the role of geography in these tales remains unexplored in his analysis.

33. Shklanka, *A Critical Edition of George Whetstone's 1583* An Heptameron of Civill Discourses, 331, citing Painter's "A Lady of Bohemia" (2.28). She is quoting from the Jacobs edition.

34. Hutson discusses this point briefly in reference to Whetstone's dramatic version of the tale (190).

35. Shklanka, *A Critical Edition of George Whetstone's 1583* An Heptameron of Civill Discourses, 245.

36. See Jeffrey Knapp, "Rogue Nationalism," *Centuries' Ends: Narrative Means,* ed. Robert D. Newman (Stanford, Calif.: Stanford Univ. Press, 1996), 140. Knapp discusses—in the context of an analysis of vagrancy and rogue literature—English fears that the Reformation would tear England apart by promoting factionalism.

37. References are by page number to the text in Charles C. Mish, ed., *Short Fiction of the Seventeenth Century* (New York: Norton, 1963). Margaret Schlauch calls this tale the "least interesting" of the narratives presented in the first version of the collection, the *Cobbler of Canterbury.* She points out that the tale is loosely based on Boccaccio 5.6, but observes that in Boccaccio's version the magnanimous king is not from Tunis, but Sicily. The French source for the tale, *Flores and Blancheflour,* contains a Saracen king. See Schlauch, "English Short Fiction in the Sixteenth and Seventeenth Centuries," 431. Boccaccio's version does not involve Tunis and is structured considerably differently. The tale does bear some relation to the fourth narrative of Barnaby Riche's *Farewell to Militarie Profession* (1581). See my discussion of it in *Fashioning Authority: The Development of Elizabethan Novelistic Discourse* (Kent, Ohio: Kent State Univ. Press, 1994), 48–54.

38. Sir Philip Sidney, *Prose Works,* ed. Albert Feuillerat (Cambridge, U.K.: Cambridge Univ. Press, 1912–26), 80–81. On the historical realities of this phenomenon,

see N. I. Matar, "'Turning Turk': Conversion to Islam in English Renaissance Thought," *Durham University Journal* (Jan. 1994): 33–41. See also Barbara Fuchs, *Mimesis and Empire: The New World, Islam, and European Identities* (Cambridge, U.K.: Cambridge Univ. Press, 2001), 118–38, for a more detailed discussion of the Christian "renegado" who converts to Islam.

3. *"Full Works to Excellent Geographers"*

1. An earlier version of portions of this essay appeared as "The Geography of the Arcadian Landscape: Constructing Otherness, Preserving Europe," in *Narrative Strategies in Early English Fiction*, ed. by Wolfgang Görtschacher and Holger Klein (Lewiston, N.Y.: Edwin Mellen, 1995), 167–86.

2. For a discussion of Sidney's explicit addresses to female readers and the implications of his construction of a female audience, see especially Hackett, *Women and Romance Fiction in the English Renaissance*, 101–15 and 113–15. See also Hutson, *The Usurer's Daughter*, 96–98.

3. See chapter 4.

4. A. C. Hamilton, "Sidney's *Arcadia* as Prose Fiction: Its Relation to Its Sources," in *Sidney in Retrospect: Selections from English Literary Renaissance*, ed. Arthur F. Kinney (Amherst: Univ. of Massachusetts Press, 1988), 124.

5. Sir Philip Sidney, *The Countess of Pembroke's Arcadia (The Old Arcadia)*, ed. Jean Robertson (Oxford, U.K.: Clarendon, 1973). All references to the text will be to this edition by page number.

6. Peter Lindenbaum, "The Geography of Sidney's *Arcadia*," *PQ* 63 (1984), 524–31.

7. Alan Sinfield, *Faultlines: Cultural Materialism and the Politics of Dissident Reading* (Berkeley: Univ. of California Press, 1992), 85.

8. Elizabeth Dipple, "Metamorphosis in Sidney's *Arcadia*," in *Essential Articles for the Study of Sir Philip Sidney*, ed. Arthur F. Kinney (Hamden, Conn.: Archon, 1986), 326.

9. Maslen, *Elizabethan Fictions*, 294–95.

10. Richard M. Berong, "Changing Attitudes Toward Material Wealth in Sidney's *Arcadias*," *Sixteenth Century Journal* 22, no. 2 (1991): 333.

11. Compare, for instance, the following passage from Markham's *The English Arcadia, Part 1* (1607), which describes Tempe. Markham borrows not only Sidney's phrasing ("well tempred myndes") but also the general emphasis on the symbolic significance of the description of the location. Note also the ethnographic dimension to the quotation that combines the description of the temple with the representation of cultural difference in reference to the "auncient Iewes Sinagogue":

This Tempe was at first called Natures Eden, because in it was no part of mans workmanship; yet the worke in Arte more stra[n]ge the[n] the Art or work of ma[n] could correct; the trees did not ouergrow one another, but seemed in euen proportions to delight in each others euennesse: the flowers did not striue which should be supreme in smelling, but comunicating their odours, were content to make one intyre sweete sauour; the beddes whereon the flowers grew, disdained not the grassie Allies, but lending to them their lustre, made the walkes more pleasant: the faire ryuer Penaus would at no time ouerflow his bankes to drowne their beauties, but with gentle swellings wash them like a deawie morning: the springs did not challenge the riuer, because his water was not as theirs, so wholesome, but paying their tribute into his bosome, made him able to beare shippes of burthen; the houses were not angrie that there were Arbors for pleasure, but shadowing the vnder their hie roofes, did safegard them from tempests? what shall I say, Tempe wanted nothing that could make it faire, yet all that it possessed made it but most beautifull, in so-much that the most famous and euer to bee admyred Prince Musidorus, after his retourne fourth of Arcadia into his Thessalia with his Pamela, in remembrance of his Shepheards life, and in honour of that life; in which he had got the honour of his contentme[n]t, taking a curious suruey both of Tempe and all her best beautyes, hee immediatlye built himselfe a moste curious house, euen in the midst thereof, where wanting nothing that might breede delight, hee found the excesse thereof did breede sometimes a loathing of pleasure, neare vnto his owne house, and round about the bordering skirts of this Tempe, hee built manye prettye and conuenient cottages; in which hee placed certaine Shepheardes whose well tempered myndes (finding the ambition of better aduaunced people, smallye auayle to the attainement of true felicitye) are the onelye schooles to teach their forrayne Neighbours, that their industrye and prouidence neyther giueth hope of disturbance, nor example of generall or priuate quarrell: into this place he would seriously retire himselfe in the voide time of his progresse, as much to renewe his remembrance with his past knowledges as to better his instant knowledge with newe matter worthye of moste excellent remembrance, so exceeding wittye were the Shepheardes by him there placed, and so much excellencye did his presence administer to them which were but simplye witted; neare vnto his owne house, hee buylt a fayre and sumptuous Temple Circular and in forme of the auncient Iewes Sinagogue the outside of marble, containing fiftie Arches, euerye Arch a dore, each dore seauen windowes, each window seauen Pyllasters of Iet, and porpherye, each pillaster. (72–73)

12. Strabo, *The Geography of Strabo,* Loeb Classical Library, 8 vols., trans. Horace Leonard Jones (New York: Putnam's, 1917), 4:27. Subsequent references to this work will be to volume and page number.

13. Thomas Floyd, *The Picture of a Perfit Common wealth . . . Gathered forth of many authors* (London, 1600), English Experience 518 (New York: Da Capo, 1971), 238. Subsequent references to Floyd's work will be by page number.

14. Robert Allott, *Wits Theater of the Little World* (London, 1599), English Experience 359 (New York: Da Capo, 1971), sig. Giv. Future references to Allott's text will be by signature number.

15. De Nicholay sig. V3^r. All future references to this work will be by signature number.

16. Dipple, "Metamorphosis in Sidney's *Arcadia*," 333.

17. For a useful discussion of several travel texts discussed in this chapter, see Parker, *Early Modern Tales of Orient*, 1–35.

18. George Abbot, *A Briefe Description of the Whole Worlde* (London, 1599), English Experience 213 (New York: Da Capo, 1970), sig. A7^r. Future references to this text will be by signature number.

19. Giovanni Botero, *The Travellers Breviat* (London, 1601), English Experience 143 (New York: Da Capo, 1969), 39. Future references to this text will by page number. It is Samuel Chew who describes Johnson's translation as an "epitome," in *The Crescent and the Rose: Islam and England During the Renaissance* (1936; repr., New York: Octagon, 1965), 8. Chew also emphasizes the popularity of the work. Botero's text was originally published in Italian between 1591 and 1596.

20. This discussion of sixteenth-century ethnographic discussions of Cyprus is adapted from my "Erasing the East from *Twelfth Night*," in *Race, Ethnicity and Power in Shakespeare and His Contemporaries*, ed. Joyce Green MacDonald (Totowa, N.J.: Farleigh Dickinson Univ. Press, 1997).

21. Sir Anthony Sherley, *Sir Anthony Sherley His Relation of His Travels into Persia* (London, 1613), English Experience 695 (New York: Da Capo, 1975), 6.

22. Vincenzo Cartari, *The Fountaine of Ancient Fiction* (London, 1599), English Experience 577 (New York: Da Capo, 1973), sig. Cciiv. Future references to this text will be by signature number.

23. Richard Hakluyt, *The Principal Navigations*, vol. 5 (Glasgow: James MacLehose and Sons, 1904), 122. Further references will be to this edition by volume and page number.

24. Andrée Thevet, *The New founde worlde, or Antarcticke* (London, 1568), English Experience 417 (New York: Da Capo, 1971), sig. Kiv. Future references to this text will be by signature number.

25. Macedon and Thessalia figure in many other Arcadian and chivalric romances in the period as well. See, for instance, Stephen Gosson's *Ephemerides of Phialo* (1579), Emanuel Forde's *Parismus* (1598), John Hind's *Eliosto Libidinoso* (1606) and *Lysimachus and Varrona* (1604), and Gervase Markham's *The English Arcadia* (1607). The references are various in significance and tone, but one seems worth noting for its linking of ethnography and fictive significance. Gosson refers to his hero, Phialo, as having been raised "like a rude *Macedon*, and taught to call a spade, a spade without any glosing" (dedication). Many other geographical locations receive only scant mention by name in the text—Asia (as a whole), "lesser Asia" (11), Syria, Mesopotamia, Paphlagonia, Lycia, and Caria. In adjectival forms, a few additional places are alluded to: Lacedemonia, Athens, Phoenicia, and (of course) Phagonia, the fictional home of the rebels against Basilius's reign. The other locations Sidney names similarly appear in a wide range of early modern romances.

26. Strabo had linked Macedonia with Thrace, not Thessalia (3.327).

27. Thomas Procter, *Of the Knowledge and Conducte of Warres* (1578), English Experience 268 (New York: Da Capo, 1970), unpaginated preface. Future references to this text will be by signature number. Although not explicitly an ethnographic work, Procter's study of warfare is studded with examples of successful and unsuccessful military strategies from a variety of cultures.

28. Johannes Boemus, *The Fardle of Facions* (London, 1555), trans. William Watreman, English Experience 227 (New York: Da Capo, 1970), sig. Piv^v. Future references to this text will be by signature number. For a more detailed discussion of Boemus's text in the history of early modern ethnographic writing, see Hodgen, *Early Anthropology in the Sixteenth and Seventeenth Centuries*, 131–43.

29. Erona's kingdom in the revised *Arcadia* is altered to Lycia, although, as Victor Stretkowicz notes, the shift in place name is not entirely consistent in Sidney's later text. Sir Philip Sidney, *The Countess of Pembroke's Arcadia (The New Arcadia)*, ed. Victor Stretkowicz (Oxford, U.K.: Clarendon, 1987), lxix.

30. Coelio Augustinus Curio, *A Notable Historie of the Saracens* (London, 1575), trans. Thomas Newton, English Experience 863 (Norwood, N.J.: Walter J. Johnson, 1977), sig. N11^r. Future references to this text will be by signature number.

31. As Samuel Chew reminds us, the "Elizabethan conception of the luxury, gorgeousness, and voluptuousness of Persian life was part of their heritage from the classical past" (234).

32. The name of the document is *A compendious and briefe declaration of the journey of M. Anth. Jenkinson, from . . . London into . . . Persia* (1563).

33. Johannes Leo (Leo Africanus), *A Geographical Historie of Africa, Written in Arabicke and Italian* (London, 1600), trans. John Pory, English Experience 133 (New York: Da Capo, 1969), 297. Further references to this work will be by page number.

34. See Franco Marenco, "Double Plot in Sidney's *Old Arcadia*," in *Essential Articles*, ed. Arthur F. Kinney, 305. Marenco argues that what readers learn is the need for repentance.

35. Salzman speculates that Greene may have seen a manuscript of *The Old Arcadia*, drawing his conclusion from a number of "minor allusions" between Greene's and Sidney's texts identified by Samuel Wolff. *English Prose Fiction*, 66. Other romances that also use Arcadia as a geographic location are John Hind's *Lysimachus and Varrona* (1604), in which the romance's lovers are driven by a storm to the Arcadian coast, where they disguise themselves as shepherds and buy a farm, and Gervase Markham's *The English Arcadia* (1607; 1613). which, it is worth noting, is set in the Thessalian city of Tempe.

36. David Margolies, *Novel and Society in Elizabethan England* (London, 1607), 135.

37. Quotations are taken from the Chadwick-Healey edition of the text (1997), which is based on the 1594 edition of the text published in London "imprinted . . . by Thomas Creede, for Thomas Woodcocke" (title page). Paul Salzman notes a link between Dickenson's and Sidney's texts, but suggests that the Arcadia of *Arisbas* "has a strong mythological content, and a delicate atmosphere. . . . [Also, it is] not threatened by political dispruption as is Sidney's. However, it is a fallen world, for it has been deserted by the Gods who once frequented it." *English Prose Fiction*, 81.

38. Ibid. Additional scholarship on Dickenson's text is scanty, but see also Kinney, who describes Dickenson's Arcadia as "a much diminished version of Sidney's" Arcadia. *Humanist Poetics,* 288.

39. Cyprus, in *Arisbas,* is the space, identified as the "noblest" of all of the islands neighboring Arcadia (14), to which the text's lovers desire to return. Arisbas and Timoclea flee Cyprus to escape resistance to their marriage, returning at the text's end to find such resistance has disappeared. Other early modern romances also treat Cyprus in a similar way—as an alternative location, an island to flee either from or to. In *Menaphon,* for example, Cyprus functions as a purely "fictional" place. It is never the site of action, and it provides only a narrative function for Sephastia, giving her the name of a place she can claim to be from, thus protecting her identity. It fulfills a function analogous to that we will observe Trapalonia providing in Greene's *Pandosto* (see chap. 4). There the fictionality of the location was immediately observed; here the geographical reality of the identified island becomes obscured and fictionalized by its remoteness from any actual function within the text.

John Hind's *Eliosto Libidinoso* (1606) also shows geographic parallels with the other Arcadian texts discussed here. It is set in Cyprus, which is initially described as a benevolent place:

> On the Ile Cyprus there reigned a king called Amasias, whose fortunate successe in warres against his foes, and bountifull curtesie towards his friends in peace, made him to be greatly feared, and loved of all men. This Amasias had to wife a Ladie called Philoclea, by birth royall, learned by education, faire by nature, by vertues famous, so that it was hard to judge whether her beauty, fortune, or vertue, wan the greatest commendations. These two linked togither in perfect love, led their lives with such fortunate content, that their subjects greatly reioyced to see their quiet disposition. They had not beene married long, but Fortune (willing to encrease their happinesse) lent them a sonne, so adorned with the gifts of Nature, as the perfection of the child greatly augmented the love of the parents, and the joy of their Commons: insomuch that the men of Cyprus to shew their inward joyes by outward actions, made Bone-fires and Triumphes throughout all the Kingdome, appointing Iustes, and Turneis, for the honor of their yong Prince: whither resorted, not onely his Nobles, but also diverse Kings and Princes, which were his neighbours, willing to divulge the friendship which they bore to Amasias, and to win fame and glorie by their prowesse and valour. (5–6)

Cyprus decays by the beginning of the second book of the romance because of the ambition its Prince. The appropriation of the name of Sidney's heroine also deserves mention, although Salzman observes that Hind also borrows from Lyly, commenting that the text's style "constantly combines echoes" of both writers. *English Prose Fiction,* 135.

40. The poems are "The Strife of Loue and Beautie," "Cvpids Palace," and "The Worth of Poesie."

4. Trapalonia, Machilenta, and the Uses of Fictional "Glasses"

1. For further discussion of Shakespeare's use of Bohemia in *The Winter's Tale*, see Richard Studing, "Shakespeare's Bohemia Revisited: A Caveat," *Shakespeare Studies* 15 (1982): 217–26; R. W. Desai, "'What Means Sicilia? He Something Seems Unsettled': Sicily, Russia, and Bohemia in *The Winter's Tale*," *Comparative Drama* 30, no. 3 (Fall 1996): 311–24; Alfonsas Šešplaukis, "Early Theories on East European Sources of Shakespeare's 'The Tempest' and 'The Winter's Tale,'" *Lituanus. Lithuanian Quarterly* 12 (1965): 45–62. See also David Snelling's "Prospero on the Coast of Bohemia," *Prospero: Rivista di Culture Anglo-Germaniche* 1 (1994): 4–16, and Rene Wellek's "Bohemia in Early English Literature," *Slavonic and East European Review* 21 (1943): 114–46, for discussion of links between Prospero and early modern Bohemian culture.

2. Josef Polišenský, "England and Bohemia in Shakespeare's Day," in *Shakespeare and His Contemporaries: Eastern and Central European Studies,* ed. Jerzy Limon and Jay L. Halio (Newark: Univ. of Delaware Press, 1993). The essay was written in 1964 and appeared originally in *Charles University on Shakespeare,* ed. Zdeněk Stříbrný (Prague: Universita Karlova, 1966), 65–81.

3. References to Greene's romance are by page number to the text as it appears in Paul Salzman, ed., *An Anthology of Elizabethan Prose Fiction* (New York: Oxford, 1987), 151–204.

4. Polišenský, "England and Bohemia in Shakespeare's Day," 191–99. Polišenský also cites John Foxe's *Acts and Monuments* as a source of information in England about Bohemia during the period. Foxe discusses the martyrdom of John Huss, Jerome of Prague, and various other Bohemian Protestant martyrs. His treatment of the deaths of these individuals contains very little generalization about the landscape or culture of Bohemia even as it describes fifteenth-century religious conflicts in the region.

5. A point also made by Snelling, "Prospero on the Coasts of Bohemia," 10–11. Snelling also discusses Bohemia's reputation for religious toleration and further asserts that the Emperor Rudolph II (1576–1612) may have served as a model for Shakespeare's Prospero (11).

6. On the other hand, Jaroslav Hornát argues that early modern English culture became much more aware of the realities of Bohemian geography so that by 1592 (in Thomas Lodge's *Euphues Shadow*) the country is described with rough geographical accuracy. See Jaroslav Hornát, "An Old Bohemian Legend in Elizabethan Literature," *Philologica Pragensia* 24 (1962): 352. See also his further development of this strain of argument in "Two Euphuistic Stories of Robert Greene: *The Carde of Fancie* and *Pandosto,*" *Philologica Pragensia* 6 (1963): 21–35.

7. See Botero, *The Travellers Breviat,* 59; Abbot, *A Briefe Description of the Whole Worlde,* sig. Aiii^v.

8. Complete title: *A Discourse Not Altogether Vnprofitable, Nor Vnpleasant for such as are desirous to know the situation and customes of forraine Cities without trauelling to see them. Containing a Discourse of all those Cities Wherein Do Flourish at this Day Priuiledged Vniversities* (London, 1600), English Experience 90 (New York: Da Capo, 1969).

9. For discussion of Moryson, though not specifically in the context of his representation of Bohemia, see Daniel J. Vitkus, "Trafficking with the Turk: English Travelers in the Ottoman Empire during the Early Seventeenth Century," in *Travel Knowledge: European "Discoveries" in the Early Modern Period,* ed. Ivo Kamps and Jyotsna Singh (New York: Palgrave, 2001), 39–40; Margaret McCurtain, "The Roots of Irish Nationalism," in *The Celtic Consciousness,* ed. Robert O'Driscoll (New York: George Braziller, 1982), 371–82; John M. Breen, "The Influence of Edmund Spenser's *View* on Fynes Moryson's *Itinerary,*" *Notes and Queries* 240 (n.s. 42), no. 3 (Sept. 1995): 363–64; Parker, *Early Modern Tales of Orient: A Critical Anthology,* 128–48; and Wellek, "Bohemia in Early English Literature," 128–33. Wellek does specifically discuss Moryson's Bohemian references.

10. Fynes Moryson, *An Itinerary . . . Conteinying His Ten Yeeres Travell Throvgh The Twelve Dominions of Germany, Bohmerland, Sweiterland, Netherland, Denmarke, Poland, Italy, Turky, France, England, Scotland, and Ireland* (London, 1617), English Experience 387 (New York: Da Capo, 1971), 1:14. Further references will be to this edition by part and page number.

11. M. Blundevile, *His Exercises, Containing Sixe Treatises* (London, 1594), English Experience 361 (New York: Da Capo, 1971).

12. Haynes, *The Humanist as Traveler,* 129.

13. See also Nancy Lindheim, who argues that even though the romance moves to Sicilia, Greene "will not fulfill our pastoral expectations. The scene will not be set among an eclogue-producing aristocracy of sheep owners." "Lyly's Golden Legacy: *Rosalynde* and *Pandosto,*" *Studies in English Literature* 15, no. 1 (1975): 17.

14. On the difficulties posed by the final sentence of the romance, see also Brenda Cantar, "'Silenced but for the Word': The Discourse of Incest in Greene's *Pandosto* and *Menaphon,*" *English Studies in Canada* 23, no. 1 (March 1997): 27–28.

15. Very little scholarly attention has been devoted to this location in Greene's text. Salzman's edition quickly dismisses it as fictional, and general scholarly opinion seems to agree with this position; however Hornát and Šešplaukis both have suggested that Trapalonia may be a corruption of "'Trans-Polonia," or the country beyond Poland, that is, Lithuania (Hornát, "Two Euphuistic Stories," 31). Both cite M. A. Biggs's "The Origin of *The Winter's Tale,*" *Notes and Queries* 12, no. 3 (1917): 164–65, as a source for this conclusion. Both scholars are part of a small tradition of seeing Greene's romance as having deep Eastern European roots. Their work seems to assume greater knowledge of Eastern European languages and traditions than seems plausible. For instance, drawing on the work of Jacob Caro (1836–1909), a German historian, on this subject, as did Biggs, they argue that "Pandosto" is itself a Slavic name, deriving from *pan* (lord) and *dostoyny* (rich). Hornát, "Two Euphuistic Stories," 31. Greene seems unlikely to have worked to create such a compound himself.

16. Interestingly, Shakespeare's Florizel increases the cultural otherness of his disguised Perdita, claiming that she is from Libya.

17. For discussions of the geography of *Pericles,* see my "Liminal Geography: *Pericles* and the Politics of Place," *Philological Quarterly* 71 (1992): 281–92.

18. Quotations from Twine are to the edition in Geoffrey Bullough's *Narrative and Dramatic Sources of Shakespeare* (New York: Columbia Univ. Press, 1966), 6:423–82. Quotations from *Pericles* are to F. D. Hoeniger's Arden Edition (New York: Routledge, 1963).

19. Qtd. in Davis, *Idea and Act in Elizabethan Fiction,* 198.

20. Other differences between the two texts that bear note, though not explicitly linked to place: the parallel between the rape of Antiochus's daughter and Apollonius as "molested in mind" by Antiochus; the presence in Twine's text of a daughter of the Lysimachus figure who is invoked as part of the reason Tharsia's arguments dissuade him from raping her but then is ignored when her father leaves Machilenta; the repetition of the letter that Apollonius includes in Lucina's casket—the contents of it are reported to us twice; the similarities between Antiochus's daughter's lament over her lost "name" and Apollonius's statement to Lucina (Shakespeare's Thaisa) after shipwrecked in Pentapolis: "Madam, if you ask my name, I have lost it in the sea" (437).

21. "Ordinances for the direction of the intended voyage for Cathay, compiled and delivered by the right worshipful Sebastian Cabot Esquire, governor of the mystery and company of the Merchant Adventurers for the discovery of regions, dominions[,] islands and places unknown, the 9th day of May, in the year of Our Lord God 1553." Hakluyt, *Voyages and Discoveries,* 58.

22. See discussion of Egypt's associations for Elizabethan readers in my "The Geography of the Arcadian Landscape: Constructing Otherness, Preserving Europe," 182–83.

23. Cantar, "'Silenced but for the Word,'" 33.

24. In Shakespeare's *Pericles,* the location of Marina's enslavement and her reunion with her father is the island of Mytilene, a clearly identifiable geographic space that has long figured in discussions of the play that attempt to link its geography to the New Testament travels of the apostle Paul and to thematic readings that see the story the play presents as about patience, familial restoration, and Christian repentance and forgiveness.

25. The map faces the beginning of Acts of the Apostles. It also locates Tyre, Antioch, and "Ephes." Mytilene and Pentapolis remain unidentified on this, one of the most common maps of the period.

26. For instance, see Watreman's translation of Boemus and many of the reports contained in *Purchas his Pilgrimes.*

5. The Ethnographic Function of Latin

1. Portions of this chapter appeared as "Humanist Learning, Eloquent Women, and the Use of Latin in Robert Greene's *Ciceronis Amor: Tullies Love,*" *Explorations in Renaissance Culture* 27, no. 1 (Summer 2001): 1–19.

2. Roger Ascham, *The Schoolmaster,* in *The Renaissance in England,* ed. Hyder E. Rollins and Herschel Baker (Lexington, Mass.: D. E. Heath, 1954), 826.

3. Ibid., 833. See Hutson, *The Usurer's Daughter* for discussion of this quotation in the context of the use of writing Italianate fiction as a means of displaying "humanistic text skills" (117).

4. Maslen, *Elizabethan Fictions,* 6.

5. From David Bevington, *The Complete Works of Shakespeare,* updated 4th ed. (New York: Longman, 1997).

6. John Hale, *The Civilization of Europe in the Renaissance* (New York: Touchstone, 1993). Benedict Anderson discusses the importance of the struggle between Latin and vernacular languages in the development of early modern European national identities in *Imagined Communities* (New York: Verso, 1991), 38–46.

7. Anon., *Lazarillo de Tormes,* in *Two Spanish Picaresque Novels,* trans. Michael Alpert (Baltimore, Md.: Penguin, 1969), 67.

8. The Latin in *Don Simonides* and *Loues Load-starre* is generally translated into English, though not always; in Nashe and Middleton, it is generally untranslated.

9. On prose fictions and other diversionary reading for women during the period, see Suzanne W. Hull, *Chaste, Silent, and Obedient: English Books for Women, 1475–1640* (San Marino, Calif.: Huntington Library, 1982), 75–82. Slightly more than half of the twenty-three books she includes in her list of "Recreational Books for Women" published between 1510 and 1603 are works of prose fiction.

10. See Lucas, *Writing for Women,* 74.

11. For a more thorough discussion of the readership of Greene's works, especially *Pandosto,* see also Newcomb's *Reading Popular Romance in Early Modern England* (New York: Columbia Univ. Press, 2002).

12. See Fleming, "The Ladies' Man and the Age of Elizabeth," 163.

13. Other texts that similarly might be considered for their intermingling of translated and untranslated Latin include William Averell's *A Dyall for Dainty Darlings* (1584), John Dickenson's *Arisbas* (1594), and Barnabe Riche's *The Adventures of Don Simonides* (1581; 1584). Stephen Gosson's *The Ephemerides of Phialo* (1579) contains an untranslated dedicatory letter to the scholars at Oxford, although it includes some translated Latin within the text itself (see 139, 180).

14. See also Amy Louise Erickson, *Women and Property in Early Modern England* (New York: Routledge, 1993), 56–59.

15. For additional discussion by Jardine of the humanist education of Italian women, see her "Isota Nogarola: Women Humanists: Education—For What?" *History of Education* 12, no. 4 (1983): 231–44.

16. Charles Crupi, *Robert Greene* (Boston: Twayne, 1986), calls it Greene's most often reprinted work (82); however, Newcomb's recent examination of the reception history of *Pandosto* calls this assessment into question. Despite its popularity, it has received little scholarly attention in the twentieth century. See my introduction to *Framing Elizabethan Fictions: Contemporary Approaches to Early Modern Narrative Prose* (Kent, Ohio: Kent State Univ. Press, 1996), 6–10; the present essay builds on material suggested there. Scholarship on the *Ciceronis Amor* also includes discussion by Reid Barbour, Elaine V. Beilin, Arthur F. Kinney, Charles W. Crupi, Phillip Parotti, David Margolies, Richard Helgerson, Charles H. Larson ("Robert Greene's

Ciceronis Amor: Fictional Biography in the Romance Genre"), Walter R. Davis, and René Pruvost.

17. It should be noted that, as Larson observes, although Nepos apparently did write a life of Cicero, it was not extant in the sixteenth century ("Robert Greene's *Ciceronis Amor,*" 257).

18. The Ennius passage: "Vnus homo nobis cunctando restituit rem, / Non ponebat enim rumores ante salutem, / Ergo postque magisque viri nunc gloria claret," *Annales* 12:360–62, is quoted in Cicero's *De Officiis* 1:24, 84. *De Officiis* was a text frequently studied by grammar schoolboys during the period. See Mary Thomas Crane, *Framing Authority: Saying, Self, and Society in Sixteenth-Century England* (Princeton, N.J.: Princeton Univ. Press, 1993), 88, and the reading lists from Tudor grammar schools included in A. Monroe Stowe, *English Grammar Schools in the Reign of Queen Elizabeth* (New York: Teachers College, Columbia University, 1908), 184–86. I am grateful to Mary E. Kuntz Pratt for her assistance with the Latin throughout this essay.

19. See Larson, "Robert Greene's *Ciceronis Amor,*" for further discussion of the romance's links to the historical and biographical novel.

20. See, for instance, in Greene's *The Royal Exchange:* "Foure thinges [which] make a man wise. (1. Studie. (2. Experience. (3. Nightly consideration. (4. And immitation of the wise." Qtd. in Kinney, *Humanist Poetics,* 186.

21. Robert Greene, *Greenes Groatsworth of Witte, Bought with a million of Repentance* (1592; repr., New York: Burt Franklin, 1970).

22. In *Kinde-Hartes Dreame,* a speech made by Robert Greene to Pierce Penniless contains several examples of untranslated Latin. See G. B. Harrison, ed., *Henrie Chettle, Kind-Hartes Dreame* (1592); *William Kemp, Nine Daies Wonder* (1600); London: The Bodley Head, (1923), 35–37. A preface to *Greene in Conceipt, spoken by Greene's ghost* also contains untranslated Latin.

23. The Latin and English versions of the letter are provided below:

Lentulus, Terentiae salutem

Quod natura in venustatis it formae tuae Idea formauit (suauissima Terentia) nullo modo silentio praeterire possum: Ne cum nimis cautus amoris ignem celare conarer, incautus tanquam Aetna meipsum consumens, in cineres redigar. Cum inter Parthos versarer, nihil nisi bellum et arma cogitans, a Roma vsque formae tuae pulchritudo, morumque integritas a multis saepe nuntiata est. Cuius rei fama ea iucunditate aures meas permulsit, vt (syrenum quasi cantu delectatus) arma abijcere et amorem cogitare coeperim, meque totum in Terentiae potestatem tradere non erubescerem. Diuinae autem excellentiae tuae cogitatio, eos mihi pro tempore in bellicis negotijs addidit animos, vt breui deuictis et profligatis Parthis, totam hanc Prouinciam Lepido commiserim, quem vnum tum honoris, tum fortunae meae participem feci, Parthisque relictis Romam me contuli, vt iucundissimo fructu tum aspectus, tum consuetudinis tuae frui liceat. Formae vero et pulchritudinis tuae dignitas, tanta tamque excellens fuit, vt non modo famam, sed expectationem meam longe superarit. Vnde exquisitam tuam perfectionem oculis contemplans, et

singulares animi dotes auribus accipiens, excellentiae tuae Idaeam in imo pectore collocaui meque totum amori, quasi constringendum tradidi. Cum igitur
tua vnius causa (suauissima Terentia) famam fortunasque et arma proiecerim,
verum amantis officium fac praestes, et me non meritis, sed amore fac metiare,
vt in amore tu mihi respondens, ego in omni officio tibi satisfaciam. Taceo
genus et parentes, quos tamen bonos ciues et senatores fuisse constat: taceo
triumphos, qui quales fuerint Capitolium populusque Romanus locupletissimi
sunt testes; de diuitijs non glorior, quas tamen mediocres esse constat, sed
virtutis vim et amoris constantiam tibi propono, quae nec parui facienda, nec
ingratitudine compensanda sunt. Me igitur fac redames (mea Terentia) et
pulchritudini comitatem coniungens, parentibus honorem, amicis fidem,
Lentulo amorem tribuas, vt parentibus gaudio, amicis vtilitati, et Lentulo
voluptati esse possis. Non diserte, vt Orator, sed peramanter, vt imperator
tibi scribo, quod si amori nostro consentire digneris, de patris voluntate nihil
est quod dubites: sed si alieno amore non nostro delecteris, dolores meos et
augebo et celabo, et quamcunque in partem te flexeris, tibi tum vitam tran-
quillam, tum mortem gloriosam, vt fidelissimus amator exoptabo. Vale, plus
oculis mihi dilecta Terentia, et me tui desiderio iam pene languentem aut
ames cito aut oderis semper, vale et rescribe. (57–58)

Lentulus to *Terentia* health.

I cannot (sweete soveraigne of my thoughts and chiefe myrrour of our *Romaine* excellencie) smother that with silence which nature hath figured in the
portraiture of my lookes, unlesse keeping the flame too secrete, I should
like *Aetna* consume to cinders. When seated amongst the *Parthians* having
nothing in my thoughtes but warres and strategemes, thy beauty was repeated as speciall newes from *Roome* amongst the Legions: The melodie
seemed so pleasing to mine eares as if the musicke of the *Syrens* had
inchaunted my senses. I ceased from warres to think of love, and from love
to doate on the conceit of *Terentia*. The thoughtes of thy excellencie doubled
such courage in my attempts, that I conquered the *Parthians,* yeelded up my
charge to *Lepidus,* made him partaker of my honors, and fortunes, and came
to *Roome* onely to see *Terentia:* whose sight was so beauteous, and so farre
beyond the report of fame, that mine eies surveying exquisitely thy perfec-
tions, and mine eares censuring of thy wit and vertues both in league con-
spired to present the Idea of thy selfe to the contemplation of my heart,
which greedily intertaining such rare beauties, hath ever since remained a
poore distressed captive. Sith then *Terentia,* thy *Lentulus* hath left his fortunes
to followe fancy, and hath forsaken the warres to winne thy loves, holding
thee more deare then country or honour, shewe thy selfe a *Romaine* Lady,
that striving in minde to be matchlesse, thou mayest bee more prodigall in
favours, then I worthy in deserts, and yeelde mee such meede for my love, as
Lentulus for his loyaltie doth merite. I boast not of my parents, they are Citizens and of the Senate with thy father. I speak not of mine honours, the

Capitol can witnes what showtes past from the *Romaines* as victors: what tears from the *Parthians* as vanquished, both these passions growing from the fortunes of *Lentulus*. My revenewes are such as satisfie my desires: But all these are externall favours, which though I rehearse yet I bragge not off. But the constancy of my love, the loyalty of my thoughts: These *Terentia* are gifts of the mind, deserving no light esteem, muche lesse to be requited with in-gratitude. Consider then (sweete goddesse) the sincerity of mine affections: weigh howe *Lentulus* loves, and so use him in love, measure his fortunes by his fancies. As thou art beautifull, so use justice, give every one his due: Honour to the gods, reverence to thy father, faith to thy friend, and Love to *Lentulus,* and if it please thee to grace me with the title, to thy husband *Lentulus:* for I covet to like honestly, not to love wantonly. I write *Terentia* as a souldier with-out eloquence, and as a lover without flattery, if thou satisfie my love with thy favours, I doubt not to seale up thy content with thy fathers and friends agree. If either thou art tied to former loves, or mislikest of mine, I will close up my sorrows with silence. Howsoever it shall please thee to returne answere: Live with content, and die with honour.
Terentias newe intertained souldier,
Publius Cornelius Lentulus (58–60)

24. Stylistic play is certainly important to this romance. Other evidence of it is seen in the obvious delight with which Greene inserts other speeches and poems into the text. The doubling of the prose and verse versions of the tale of the love of Phillis and Coridon provide the most striking example of how much Greene is interested in playing with genres and styles within this work. All of the other texts inserted into the romance—speeches, poems, songs, letters, and even an episode drawn from Boccaccio—are presented in English, not Latin. Parotti's essay, "Hav-ing it Both Ways: Renaissance Traditions in Robert Greene's 'Mars and Venus,'" *Explorations in Renaissance Culture* 12 (1986): 46–57, focuses entirely on one such embedded poem.

25. At least one sentence in the letter under discussion (*"Me igitur fac . . . "* [58]) is so markedly Ciceronian that it seems nearly to parody Cicero's style. It seems quite likely that the author would have intended his readers to have noticed the sentence's parodic qualities.

26. A further observation about this quotation deserves mention: I have not included the construction "verbatim worde for worde" as an instance of translated Latin within the text for two reasons: the OED lists *verbatim* as having been used as an English word since 1481, and Greene's text does not print the word, as it does instances of inserted Latin, in italic type.

27. Richard Helgerson, *The Elizabethan Prodigals* (Berkeley: Univ. of California Press, 1976), 94–95. Greene describes *Mamillia* as a text "wherin with perpetual fame the constancy of gentlewomen is canonized and the unjust blasphemes of women's supposed fickleness (breathed out by divers injurious persons) by manifest examples clearly infringed" (qtd. 82). Yet the tension between his concern for the representa-

tion of women and his humanist training is present even in this, his first publication. As Kinney writes of *Mamillia:* "In transporting his explorations of man's educability and perfectability to strange lands, Greene means to keep the concerns of Tudor humanism squarely before us. Indeed in grafting the marvels of Ovid and of Alexandrian romance to the conservative moral tenets of humanism, Greene seems anxious from the first to declare his allegiance to the New Learning." *Humanist Poetics,* 184.

28. The power of her rhetorical style may also reflect the dissatisfaction that some humanists felt with the heavy influence of Ciceronianism. Kristian Jensen, "The Humanist Reform of Latin and Latin Teaching," in *The Cambridge Companion to Renaissance Humanism,* ed. Jill Kraye (Cambridge, Cambridge Univ. Press, 1996), 75–76.

Conclusion

1. In the anonymous Frederyke of Jennen (1560?), the tale is set in France, and the merchants come from France, Spain, Florence, and Jennen. It is the King of Cairo who provides the political protection for the disguised wife (see Bullough). Fenton and Pettie also include analogues in their novella collections.

2. It might be worth exploring the issue of tribute in *Cymbeline* as well in relation to the version of the tale as presented in *Smelts:* Edward IV exacted tribute from Louis XI of France; the paying of tribute to Rome is, of course, a significant element in Shakespeare's play.

3. Quotations from this tale are taken from the 1620 translation of it, included in the Signet Classic edition of the play. The year 1620 alone seems to have been an important one in England for this story.

4. See Jean E. Howard, "Women, Foreigners, and the Regulation of Urban Space in *Westward Ho,*" in *Material London, ca. 1600,* ed. Lena Cowen Orlin (Philadelphia: Univ. of Pennsylvania Press, 2000), 151. She also notes that Brainford "is the conventional place beyond the immediate London suburbs where gallants and city wives go to outwit jealous husbands" in many texts during the period (161).

5. Stephen Inwood, *A History of London,* rev. ed. (London: Papermac, 2000), 125.

6. John Stowe, *The Survey of London* (London: Dent, 1912), 193.

Works Cited

Abbot, George. *A Briefe Description of the Whole Worlde.* London, 1599. The English Experience 213. New York: Da Capo, 1970.

Allott, Robert. *Wits Theater of the Little World.* London, 1599. The English Experience 359. New York: Da Capo, 1971.

Alpert, Michael, trans. *Lazarillo de Tormes.* In *Two Spanish Picaresque Novels,* 21–81. Baltimore, Md.: Penguin, 1969.

Anderson, Benedict. *Imagined Communities.* New York: Verso, 1991.

Ascham, Roger. *The Scholemaster.* In *The Renaissance in England,* ed. Hyder E. Rollins and Herschel Baker, 817–40. Lexington, Mass.: D. C. Heath, 1954.

Averell, William. *Dyall for Dainty Darlings rockt in the cradle of Securitie: A Glasse for all disobedient Sonnes to looke in. A Myrrour for vertuous Maydes. A Booke right excellent, garnished with many woorthy examples, and learned aucthorities, most needefull for this tyme present.* London, 1584. Early English Prose Fiction Full-Text Database. STC978. Cambridge, U.K.: Chadwick-Healey, 1997.

Barbour, Reid. *Deciphering Elizabethan Fiction.* Newark: Univ. of Delaware Press, 1993.

Bartels, Emily. "Making More of the Moor: Aaron, Othello, and Renaissance Refashionings of Race." *Shakespeare Quarterly* 41, no. 4 (Winter 1990): 433–54.

Beilin, Elaine V. *The Uses of Mythology in Elizabethan Prose Romance.* New York: Garland, 1988.

Berong, Richard M. "Changing Attitudes toward Material Wealth in Sidney's *Arcadias.*" *Sixteenth Century Journal* 22, no. 2 (1991): 331–49.

Bhabha, Homi. *His Exercises, Containing Sixe Treatises.* London, 1594. The English Experience 361. New York: Da Capo, 1971.

———. *The Location of Culture.* New York: Routledge, 1994.

Biggs, M. A. "The Origin of *The Winter's Tale.*" *Notes and Queries* 12, no. 3 (1917): 164–65.

Blanton, Casey. *Travel Writing: The Self and the World.* New York: Twayne, 1997.

Blundeville, Thomas. *Brief Description of Universal Maps and Cards.* London, 1589. The English Experience 438. New York: Da Capo, 1972.

Boemus, Johannes. *The Fardle of Facions.* London, 1555. Trans. William Watreman. The English Experience 227. New York: Da Capo, 1970.

Boesky, Amy. *Founding Fictions: Utopias in Early Modern England.* Athens: Univ. of Georgia Press, 1996.

Botero, Giovanni. *The Travellers Breviat.* London, 1601. The English Experience 143. New York: Da Capo, 1969.

Breen, John M. "The Influence of Edmund Spenser's *View* on Fynes Moryson's *Itinerary.*" *Notes and Queries* 240 (n.s. 42), no. 3 (Sept. 1995): 363–64.

Cantar, Brenda. "'Silenced but for the Word': The Discourse of Incest in Greene's *Pandosto* and *Menaphon.*" *English Studies in Canada* 23, no. 1 (March 1997): 27–28.

Cartari, Vincenzo. *The Fountaine of Ancient Fiction.* London, 1599. The English Experience 577. New York: Da Capo, 1973.

Cavendish, Margaret. *The Description of a New World Called the Blazing World.* In *An Anthology of Seventeenth-Century Fiction,* ed. Paul Salzman, 249–348. Oxford, U.K.: Oxford Univ. Press, 1991.

Chew, Samuel. *The Crescent and the Rose: Islam and England during the Renaissance.* 1936. Repr. New York: Octagon, 1965.

Cholakian, Patricia Francis. *Rape and Writing in the* Heptameron *of Marguerite de Navarre.* Carbondale: Southern Illinois Univ. Press, 1991.

Collins, Jane. "Publishing Private Pleasures: The Gentlewoman Reader of Barnaby Riche and George Pettie." *Explorations in Renaissance Culture* 22, no. 2 (Winter 2003): 185–210.

Coryate, Thomas. *Greetings from the Court of the Great Mogul.* London, 1616. The English Experience 30. New York: Da Capo, 1968.

Coverte, Robert. *A True and Almost Incredible Report of an Englishman.* 1612. The English Experience 302. New York: Da Capo, 1971.

Crane, Mary Thomas. *Framing Authority: Saying, Self, and Society in Sixteenth-Century England.* Princeton, N.J.: Princeton Univ. Press, 1993.

Crane, Thomas F. *Italian Social Customs of the Sixteenth Century and Their Influence on the Literature of Europe.* New Haven, Conn.: Yale Univ. Press, 1920.

Cressy, David. *Literacy and the Social Order: Reading and Writing in Tudor and Stuart England.* Cambridge, U.K.: Cambridge Univ. Press, 1980.

Crupi, Charles W. *Robert Greene.* Boston, Mass.: Twayne, 1986.

Cuningham, William. *The Cosmographical Glasse conteinyng the pleasant Principles of Cosmographie, Geographie, Hydrographie, or Nauigation.* London, 1559. The English Experience 44. New York: Da Capo, 1968.

Curio, Coelio Augustinus. *A Notable Historie of the Saracens.* Trans. Thomas Newton. London, 1575. The English Experience 863. Norwood, N.J.: Walter J. Johnson, 1977.

Dathorne, O. R. *Imagining the World: Mythical Belief versus Reality in Global Encounters.* Westport, Conn.: Bergin and Garvey, 1994.

Davis, Lennard J. *Factual Fictions: The Origins of the English Novel.* New York: Columbia Univ. Press, 1983.

Davis, Walter R. *Idea and Act in Elizabethan Fiction.* Princeton, N.J.: Princeton Univ. Press, 1969.

De Certeau, Michel. *The Practice of Everyday Life.* Trans. Steven F. Rendall. Berkeley: Univ. of California Press, 1984.

De Navarre, Marguerite. *The Heptameron.* Trans. and ed. P. A. Chilton. New York: Viking Penguin, 1984.

De Nicholay, Nicholas. *The Navigations, Peregrinations and Voyages, made into Turkie.* London, 1585. The English Experience 48. New York: Da Capo, 1968.

Desai, R. W. "'What Means Sicilia? He Something Seems Unsettled': Sicily, Russia, and Bohemia in *The Winter's Tale.*" *Comparative Drama* 30, no. 3 (Fall 1996): 311–24.

De Somogyi, Nick. "Marlowe's Maps of War." In *Christopher Marlowe and English Renaissance Culture,* ed. Daryll Grantley and Peter Roberts, 96–109. Aldershot, U.K.: Scolar, 1996.

Dickenson, John. *Arisbas.* London 1594. Early English Prose Fiction Full-Text Database. STC6817. Cambridge, U.K.: Chadwick-Healey, 1997.

Dipple, Elizabeth. "Metamorphosis in Sidney's *Arcadia.*" In *Essential Articles for the Study of Sir Philip Sidney,* ed. Arthur F. Kinney, 326–45. Hamden, Conn.: Archon, 1986.

Donovan, Josephine. *Women and the Rise of the Novel, 1405–1726.* New York: St. Martin's, 1999.

Ellman, Richard, and Robert O'Clair, eds. *The Norton Anthology of Modern Poetry.* New York: Norton, 1973.

Erickson, Amy Louise. *Women and Property in Early Modern England.* New York: Routledge, 1993.

Fenton, Geoffrey. *Certain Tragical Discourses of Bandello.* 2 vols. 1898. Repr. New York: AMS, 1967.

Fleming, Juliet. "The Ladies' Man and the Age of Elizabeth." In *Sexuality and Gender in Early Modern Europe: Institutions, Texts, Images,* ed. James Grantham Turner, 158–81. Cambridge, U.K.: Cambridge Univ. Press, 1993.

Floyd, Thomas. *The Picture of a Perfit Common wealth . . . gathered forth of many authors.* London, 1600. The English Experience 518. New York: Da Capo, 1971.

Fuchs, Barbara. *Mimesis and Empire: The New World, Islam, and European Identities.* Cambridge, U.K.: Cambridge Univ. Press, 2001.

Gascoigne, George. "The Adventures of Master FJ." In *A Hundreth Sundrie Flowres.* 1573. Early English Prose Fiction Full-Text Database. STC11635.

Gillies, John. *Shakespeare and the Geography of Difference.* Cambridge, U.K.: Cambridge Univ. Press, 1994.

Gosson, Stephen. *The Ephemerides of Phialo.* London, 1579. Early English Prose Fiction Full-Text Database. STC12093.

Grafton, Anthony. *New Worlds, Ancient Texts: The Power of Tradition and the Shock of Discovery.* Cambridge, Mass.: Belknap, 1992.

Grange, John. *The Golden Aphroditis and Grange's Garden.* New York: Scholars' Facsimiles and Reprints, 1939.

Greenblatt, Stephen. *Marvelous Possessions: The Wonder of the New World.* Chicago: Univ. of Chicago Press, 1991.

Greene, Robert. *A Critical Edition of Robert Greene's* Ciceronis Amor: Tullies Love. Ed. Charles Howard Larson. Salzburg: Institut fur Englische Sprache und Literatur, 1974.

———. *Greene's Groatsworth of Witte, Bought with a million of Repentance.* London, 1592. New York: Burt Franklin, 1970.

———. *Menaphon.* London, 1589.

———. *A Notable Discovery of Cozenage.* In *Rogues, Vagabonds, and Sturdy Beggars,* ed. Arthur F. Kinney, 163–86. Amherst: Univ. of Massachusetts Press, 1990.

Hackett, Helen. *Women and Romance Fiction in the English Renaissance.* Cambridge, U.K.: Cambridge Univ. Press, 2000.

Hakluyt, Richard. *The Principal Navigations.* 1589. Glasgow, Scot.: James MacLehose and Sons, 1904.

———. *Voyages and Discoveries.* Ed. Jack Beeching. New York: Penguin, 1972.

Hale, John. *The Civilization of Europe in the Renaissance.* New York: Touchstone, 1993.

Hamilton, A. C. "Sidney's *Arcadia* as Prose Fiction: Its Relation to Its Sources." In *Sidney in Retrospect: Selections from English Literary Renaissance,* ed. Arthur F. Kinney, 119–50. Amherst: Univ. of Massachusetts Press, 1988.

Hampton, Timothy. *Literature and Nation in the Sixteenth Century: Inventing Renaissance France.* Ithaca, N.Y.: Cornell Univ. Press, 2001.

———. *Writing from History: The Rhetoric of Exemplarity in Renaissance Literature.* Ithaca, N.Y.: Cornell Univ. Press, 1990.

Harriot, Thomas. *A Briefe and True Report of the New Found Land of Virginia.* 1590. New York: Dover, 1972.

Harrison, G. B., ed. *Henrie Chettle, Kind-Hartes Dreame (1592); William Kemp, Nine Daies Wonder (1600).* London: Bodley Head, 1923.

Haynes, Jonathan. *The Humanist as Traveler: George Sandys' Relation of a Journey begun An. Dom. 1619.* Rutherford, N.J.: Farleigh Dickinson Univ. Press, 1986.

Helgerson, Richard. *The Elizabethan Prodigals.* Berkeley: Univ. of California Press, 1976.

———. "Writing Empire and Nation." In *The Cambridge Companion to English Literature, 1500–1600,* ed. Arthur F. Kinney, 310–29. Cambridge, U.K.: Cambridge Univ. Press, 2000.

Hind, John. *Eliosto Libidinoso.* London, 1606. Early English Prose Fiction Full-Text Database. STC13509.

———. *Lysimachus and Varrona.* London,1604. Early English Prose Fiction Full-Text Database. STC13510.

Hodgen, Margaret. *Early Anthropology in the Sixteenth and Seventeenth Centuries.* Philadelphia: Univ. of Pennsylvania Press, 1964.

Hoffman, Ann. *Lives of the Tudor Age.* New York: Barnes and Noble, 1977.

Holinshed, Raphael. *Chronicles of England, Scotland, and Ireland.* 1577–1587; 1807. Repr. New York: AMS, 1965.

Hornát, Jaroslav. "An Old Bohemian Legend in Elizabethan Literature." *Philologica Pragensia* 24 (1962): 345–52.

————. "Two Euphuistic Stories of Robert Greene: *The Carde of Fancie* and *Pandosto.*" *Philologica Pragensia* 6 (1963): 21–35.

Howard, Jeane. "Women, Foreigners, and the Regulation of Urban Space in *Westward Ho.*" In *Material London, ca. 1600,* ed. Lena Cowen Orlin, 150–67. Philadelphia: Univ. of Pennsylvania Press, 2000.

Hull, Suzanne. *Chaste, Silent, and Obedient: English Books for Women, 1475–1640.* San Marino, Calif.: Huntington Library, 1982.

Hutson, Lorna. *The Usurer's Daughter: Male Friendship and Fictions of Women in Sixteenth-Century England.* New York: Routledge, 1994.

Inwood, Stephen. *A History of London.* Rev. ed. London: Papermac, 2000.

Jardine, Lisa. "Isota Nogarola: Women Humanists: Education—For What?" *History of Education* 12, no. 4 (1983): 231–44.

————. "'O Decus Italiae Virgo,' or The Myth of the Learned Lady in the Renaissance." *Historical Journal* 28 (1985): 799–819.

Jensen, Kristian. "The Humanist Reform of Latin and Latin Teaching." In *The Cambridge Companion to Renaissance Humanism,* ed. Jill Kraye, 63–81. Cambridge, U.K.: Cambridge Univ. Press, 1996.

Jones, Ann Rosalind, and Peter Stallybrass. "Dismantling Irena: The Sexualizing of Ireland in Early Modern England." In *Nationalisms and Sexualities,* ed. Andrew Parker, Mary Russo, Doris Sommer, and Patricia Yaeger, 157–71. New York: Routledge, 1992.

King. Margaret L. *Women of the Renaissance.* Chicago: Univ. of Chicago Press, 1991.

Kinney, Arthur F. *Humanist Poetics: Thought, Rhetoric, and Fiction in Sixteenth-Century England.* Amherst: Univ. of Massachusetts Press, 1986.

————. "Situational Poetics." *Prose Studies* 11, no. 2 (Sept. 1988), 10–24.

Kintgen, Eugene R. "Reconstructing the Interpretive Conventions of Elizabethan Readers." In *Language, Text and Context: Essays in Stylistics,* ed. Michael Toolan, 93–107. New York: Routledge, 1992.

Knapp, Jeffrey. *An Empire Nowhere: England, America, and Literature from Utopia to the Tempest.* Berkeley: Univ. of California Press, 1992.

————. "Rogue Nationalism." In *Centuries' Ends: Narrative Means,* ed. Robert D. Newman, 138–50. Stanford, Calif.: Stanford Univ. Press, 1996.

Kristeva, Julia. *Strangers to Ourselves.* Trans. Leon S. Roudiez. New York: Columbia Univ. Press, 1991.

Lach, Donald F., and Theodore Nicholas Foss. "Images of Asia and Asians in European Fiction, 1500–1800." In *Asia in Western Fiction,* ed. Robin W. Winks and James R. Rush, 14–34. Honolulu: Univ. of Hawaii Press, 1990.

Langer, Ullrich. "The Renaissance Novella as Justice." *Renaissance Quarterly* 52, no. 2 (Summer 1999): 311–41.

Larson, Charles H. "Robert Greene's *Ciceronis Amor:* Fictional Biography in the Romance Genre." *Studies in the Novel* 6 (1974): 256–67.

Leo, Johannes (Leo Africanus). *A Geographical Historie of Africa, Written in Arabicke and Italian.* London, 1600. Trans. John Pory. The English Experience 133. New York: Da Capo, 1969.

Lestringant, Frank. *Cannibals: The Discovery and Representation of the Cannibal from Columbus to Jules Verne.* Trans. Rosemary Morris. Berkeley: Univ. of California Press, 1997.

Lewkenor, Samuel. *A Discourse Not Altogether Vnprofitable, Nor Vnpleasant for such as are desirous to know the situation and customes of forraine Cities without trauelling to see them. Containing a Discourse of all those Cities Wherein Do Flourish at this Day Priuiledged Vniversities.* London, 1600. The English Experience 90. New York: Da Capo, 1969.

Lindenbaum, Peter. "The Geography of Sidney's *Arcadia.*" *Philological Quarterly* 63 (1984): 524–31.

Lindheim, Nancy. "Lyly's Golden Legacy: *Rosalynde* and *Pandosto.*" *Studies in English Literature* 15, no. 1 (1975): 3–20.

Linton, Joan Pong. "The Humanist in the Market: Gendering Exchange and Authorship in Lyly's *Euphues* Romances." In *Framing Elizabethan Fictions*, ed. Constance C. Relihan, 73–97. Kent, Ohio: Kent State Univ. Press, 1996.

Lithgow, William. *A Most Delectable, and Trve Discourse, of an admired and painefull peregrination from Scotland, to the most famous Kingdomes in Europe, Asia, and Affricke.* 1614. The English Experience 399. New York: Da Capo, 1971.

Lodge, Thomas. *Rosalind. Euphues' Golden Legacy Found after His Death in His Cell at Silexedra.* 1590. Ed. Donald Beecher. Ottawa, Can.: Dovehouse, 1997.

Lucas, Caroline. *Writing for Women: The Example of Woman as Reader in Elizabethan Romance.* Philadelphia, Pa.: Open Univ. Press, 1989.

Lyly, John. *The Complete Works of John Lyly.* 1902. Ed. R. Warwick Bond. Repr. Oxford, U.K.: Clarendon, 1967.

Marenco, Franco. "Double Plot in Sidney's *Old Arcadia.*" In *Essential Articles for the Study of Sir Philip Sidney,* ed. Arthur F. Kinney, 287–310. Hamden, Conn.: Archon, 1986.

Margolies, David. *Novel and Society in Elizabethan England.* London: Croom Helm, 1985.

Markham, Gervase. *The English Arcadia.* Part 1. London, 1607. Early English Prose Fiction Full-Text Database. STC17351.

Maslen, R. W. *Elizabethan Fictions: Espionage, Counter-Espionage and the Duplicity of Fiction in Early Elizabethan Prose Narratives.* Oxford, U.K.: Clarendon, 1997.

Matar, N. I. "'Turning Turk': Conversion to Islam in English Renaissance Thought." *Durham University Journal* (Jan. 1994): 33–41.

McCurtain, Margaret. "The Roots of Irish Nationalism." In *The Celtic Consciousness,* ed. Robert O'Driscoll, 371–82. New York: George Braziller, 1982.

Melbanke, Brian. *Philotimus.* London, 1582. Early English Prose Fiction Full-Text Database. STC17801.

Mish, Charles C., ed. *Short Fiction of the Seventeenth Century.* New York: Norton, 1963.

Moryson, Fynes. *An Itinerary . . . Conteinying His Ten Yeeres Travell Throvgh The Twelve Dominions of Germany, Bohmerland, Sweiterland, Netherland, Denmarke, Poland, Italy, Turky, France, England, Scotland, and Ireland.* London, 1617. The English Experience 387. New York: Da Capo, 1971.

Nashe, Thomas. *The Complete Works of Thomas Nashe.* Ed. R. B. McKerrow. Repr. Oxford, U.K.: Blackwell, 1958.

Nelson, William. *Fact or Fiction: The Dilemma of the Renaissance Storyteller.* Cambridge, Mass.: Harvard Univ. Press, 1973.

Neville-Singleton, Pamela. "'A Very Good Trumpet': Richard Hakluyt and the Politics of Overseas Expansion." In *Texts and Cultural Change in Early Modern England,* ed. Cedric C. Brown and Arthur Marotti, 66–79. New York: St. Martin's, 1997.

Newcomb, Lori Humphrey. *Reading Popular Romance in Early Modern England.* New York: Columbia Univ. Press, 2002.

———. "The Romance of Service: The Simple History of *Pandosto*'s Servant Readers." In *Framing Elizabethan Fictions,* ed. Relihan, 117–39.

Newton, Thomas, trans. Coelio Augustinus Curio, *A Notable Historie of the Saracens.* London, 1575. The English Experience 863. Norwood, N.J.: Walter J. Johnson, 1977.

Painter, William. *The Palace of Pleasure.* 4 vols. London: Cresset, 1929.

Parker, Kenneth ed. *Early Modern Tales of Orient: A Critical Anthology.* New York: Routledge, 1999.

Parotti, Phillip. "Having it Both Ways: Renaissance Traditions in Robert Greene's 'Mars and Venus.'" *Explorations in Renaissance Culture* 12 (1986): 46–57.

Pettie, George. *A Petite Palace of Pettie His Pleasure.* Ed. Herbert Hartman. London: Oxford Univ. Press, 1938.

Polišenský, Josef. "England and Bohemia in Shakespeare's Day." In *Shakespeare and His Contemporaries: Eastern and Central European Studies,* ed. Jerzy Limon and Jay L. Halio, 189–204. Newark: Univ. of Delaware Press, 1993.

Prendergast, Maria Teresa Michaela. *Renaissance Fantasies: The Gendering of Aesthetics in Early Modern Fiction.* Kent, Ohio: Kent State Univ. Press, 1999.

Procter, Thomas. *Of the Knowledge and Conducte of Warres.* London, 1578. The English Experience 268. New York: Da Capo, 1970.

Pruvost, René. *Matteo Bandello and Elizabethan Fiction.* Paris: Librarie Ancienne Honoré Champion, 1937.

———. *Robert Greene et ses Romans (1558–1592).* Paris: Societé d'Edition "Les Belles Lettre," 1938.

Purchas, Samuel. *Hakluytus Posthumous or Purchas His Pilgrimes.* 1624.

———. *Purchas His Pilgrimage or Relations of the World and the Religions Obserued in Al Ages and Places Discouered, from the Creation to the Present.* 1613.

Rabelais, François. *The Works of Rabelais.* Trans. Sir Thomas Urquhart and Peter Anthony Matteux. London: Bullen, 1904.

Raleigh, Sir Walter. *Sir Walter Raleigh: Selected Writings.* Ed. Gerald Hammond. Manchester, U.K.: Carcanet, 1984.

Relihan, Constance C. "Erasing the East from *Twelfth Night.*" In *Race, Ethnicity and Power in Shakespeare and His Contemporaries,* ed. Joyce Green MacDonald, 80–94. Totowa, N.J.: Farleigh Dickinson Univ. Press, 1997.

———. *Fashioning Authority: The Development of Elizabethan Novelistic Discourse.* Kent, Ohio: Kent State Univ. Press, 1994.

———. "The Geography of the Arcadian Landscape: Constructing Otherness, Preserving Europe." In *Narrative Strategies in Early English Fiction,* ed. Wolfgang Gortschacher and Holger Klein, 169–86. Lewiston, N.Y.: Edwin Mellen, 1995.

———. "Humanist Learning, Eloquent Women, and the Use of Latin in Robert Greene's *Ciceronis Amor: Tullies Love.*" *Explorations on Renaissance Culture* 27, no. 1 (Summer 2001): 1–19.

———. Introduction to *Framing Elizabethan Fictions,* ed. Relihan, 1–15.

———. "Liminal Geography: *Pericles* and the Politics of Place." *Philological Quarterly* 71 (1992): 281–92.

———, and Goran V. Stanivukovic, eds. *Prose Fiction and Early Modern Sexualities in England, 1570–1640.* New York: Palgrave Macmillan, 2003.

Richardson, Laurel, and Ernest Lockridge. "Fiction and Ethnography: A Conversation. Part 2." *Quarterly Inquiry* 4, no. 3 (Sept. 1998): 328–37.

Riche, Barnabe. *His Farewell to Military Profession.* Ed. Donald Beecher. Ottawa, Can.: Dovehouse, 1992.

———. *The Aventures of Don Simonides.* London, 1581; 1584. Early English Prose Fiction Full-Text Database. STC21002; STC21002a.

Robarts, Henry. *Honours Conquest.* London, 1598. Early English Prose Fiction Full-Text Database. STC21082.

———. *Pheander the Mayden Knight.* London, 1595. Early English Prose Fiction Full-Text Database. STC21087.

Salzman, Paul. *English Prose Fiction, 1558–1700: A Critical History.* Oxford, U.K.: Oxford Univ. Press, 1985.

———, ed. *An Anthology of Elizabethan Prose Fiction.* New York: Oxford, 1987.

Sandys, George. *A Relation of a Iourney begun An: Dom: 1610. Fovre Bookes Containing a description of the Turkish Empire, of Ægypt, of the Holy Land, of the Remote parts of Italy, and Ilands adioyning.* 2d ed. 1615. The English Experience 554. New York: Da Capo, 1973.

Schlauch, Margaret. "English Short Fiction in the Fifteenth and Sixteenth Centuries." *Studies in Short Fiction* 3 (1966): 393–434.

Schleiner, Winfried. "Cross-Dressing, Gender Errors, and Sexual Taboos in Renaissance Literature." In *Gender Reversals and Gender Cultures,* ed. Sabrina Petra Ramet, 92–104. New York: Routledge, 1996.

Šešplaukis, Alfonsas. "Early Theories on East European Sources of Shakespeare's 'The Tempest' and 'The Winter's Tale.'" *Lituanus Lithuanian Quarterly* 12 (1965): 45–62.

Shakespeare, William. *The Norton Shakespeare.* Ed. Stephen Greenblatt, et al. New York: Norton, 1997.

Sherley, Sir Anthony. *Sir Anthony Sherley His Relation of His Travels into Persia.* London, 1613. The English Experience 695. New York: Da Capo, 1975.

Sidney, Sir Philip. *The Countess of Pembroke's Arcadia (The New Arcadia).* Ed. Victor Stretkowicz. Oxford, U.K.: Clarendon, 1987.

———. *The Countess of Pembroke's Arcadia (The Old Arcadia).* Ed. Jean Robertson. Oxford, U.K.: Clarendon, 1973.

————. *Prose Works.* 4 vols. Ed. Albert Feuillerat. Cambridge, U.K.: Cambridge Univ. Press, 1912–26.

Sinfield, Alan. *Faultlines: Cultural Materialism and the Politics of Dissident Reading.* Berkeley: Univ. of California Press, 1992.

Smarr, Janet Levarie, trans. *Italian Renaissance Tales.* Rochester, Mich.: Solaris, 1983.

Snader, Joe. *Caught between Worlds: British Captivity Narratives in Fact and Fiction.* Lexington: Univ. Press of Kentucky, 2000.

Snelling, David. "Prospero on the Coast of Bohemia." *Prospero: Rivista di Culture Anglo-Germaniche* 1 (1994): 4–16.

Spufford, Margaret. *Small Books and Pleasant Histories: Popular Fiction and its Readership in Seventeenth-Century England.* New York: Methuen, 1981.

Stowe, A. Monroe. *English Grammar Schools in the Reign of Queen Elizabeth.* New York: Teachers College Columbia University, 1908.

Stowe, John. *The Survey of London.* London: Dent, 1912.

Strabo. *The Geography of Strabo.* Trans. Horace Leonard Jones. 8 vols. Loeb Classical Library. New York: Putnam's, 1917.

Studing, Richard. "Shakespeare's Bohemia Revisited: A Caveat." *Shakespeare Studies* 15 (1982): 217–26.

Taylor, E. G. R. *Late Tudor and Early Stuart Geography, 1583–1650.* London: Methuen, 1934.

Tetel, Marcel. *Marguerite de Navarre's* Heptameron: *Themes, Language, and Structure.* Durham, N.C.: Duke Univ. Press, 1973.

Thevet, André. *The New Found Worlde, or Antarticke.* 1568. The English Experience 417. New York: Da Capo, 1971.

Twine, Lawrence. *The Patterne of Painefull Adventures.* In *Narrative and Dramatic Sources of Shakespeare,* vol. 6, ed. Geoffrey Bullough, 423–82. New York: Columbia Univ. Press, 1966.

Vitkus, Daniel J. "Trafficking with the Turk: English Travelers in the Ottoman Empire during the Early Seventeenth Century." In *Travel Knowledge: European "Discoveries" in the Early Modern Period,* ed. Ivo Kamps and Jyotsna Singh, 35–52. New York: Palgrave, 2001.

Waddington, Raymond. "Rewriting the World, Rewriting the Body." In *The Cambridge Companion to English Literature, 1500–1600,* ed. Arthur F. Kinney, 287–309. Cambridge, U.K.: Cambridge Univ. Press, 2000.

Washington, T. *The Nauigations, Peregrinations, and Voyages, made into Turkie by Nicholas Nicholay Daulphinois, Lord of Arfeiule, Chamberlaine and Geographer ordinarie to the King of Fraunce: conteining sundry singularities which the Author hath there seene and obserued.* 1585. The English Experience 48. New York: Da Capo, 1968.

Watson, Foster, ed. *Vives and the Renascence Education of Women.* New York: Longmans, Green and Company, 1912.

Wellek, Rene. "Bohemia in Early English Literature." *Slavonic and East European Review* 21 (1943): 114–46.

Westward for Smelts: An Early Collection of Stories. Ed. James Orchard Halliwell. London: Percy Society, 1848.

Whetstone, George. *A Critical Edition of George Whetstone's 1582* An Heptameron of Civill Discourses. Ed. Diana Shklanka. New York: Garland, 1987.

———. *The English Myrror.* 1586. The English Experience 632. New York: Da Capo, 1973.

Wilson, K. J. *Incomplete Fictions: The Formation of English Renaissance Dialogue.* Washington, D.C.: Catholic Univ. Press, 1985.

Wilson, Richard. "Voyage to Tunis: New History and the Old World of *The Tempest*," *ELH* 64, 2 (Summer 1997): 333–57.

Wright, Louis B. "Henry Robarts: Patriotic Propagandist and Novelist." *Studies in Philology* 29 (1932): 176–99.

Index

DATE DUE			

GAYLORD No. 2333   PRINTED IN U.S.A.